PRESS *press*

PAUSE *pause*

THE BREAKDOWN THAT REBUILT MY LIFE & CHANGED A FAMILY LEGACY

PRESS PAUSE

MAUREEN
SPATARO

inspired *girl* BOOKS

Press Pause by Maureen Spataro
Published by Inspired Girl Books
821 Belmar Plaza, Unit 5 Belmar, NJ 07719
www.inspiredgirlbooks.com

Inspired Girl Books is honored to bring forth books with heart and stories that matter. We are proud to offer this book to our readers; the story, the experiences, and the words are the author's alone.

The events are portrayed to the best of the author's memory. While all the stories in this book are true, some names and identifying details have been changed to protect the privacy of the people involved.

The author has tried to recreate events, locales, and conversations from her memories of them. In order to maintain their anonymity in some instances she has changed the names of individuals and places, she may have changed some identifying characteristics and details such as physical properties, occupations, and places of residence.

The conversations in the book all come from the author's recollections, though they are not written to represent word-for-word transcripts. Rather, the author has retold them in a way that evokes the feeling and meaning of what was said. In all instances, the essence of the dialogue is accurate.

The author and publisher do not assume and hereby disclaim any liability in connection with the use of the information contained in this book.

ISBN: 978-0-578-65932-9
Cover Illustration by Roseanna White Designs
Editing by Colella Communications, Inspired Girl Books, and Janelle Leonard
Author photograph by Mary Foti of Nautical Media Group

Library of Congress Control Number:
2020903878

Contents

A Note from the Author

This story is real. This story is difficult. But, this story is not unique. So many people struggle with the shame and guilt brought on by the secrets they hide. Coupled with fear of being judged, or not believed, it's a heavy and almost impossible burden to carry alone. My greatest wish is that those who live in silence recognize the strength and resilience they possess, and find pride in being a survivor. In addition, I hope those who love and support them understand the vital role they can play in helping their loved one heal.

For Linda

"You're a warrior with a fragile soul, Maureen.
90% of your success is just showing up."

I remember your words, and I show up . . .
even on my most difficult days.

With love and thanks always.

Introduction

AS A CHILD, RELIGION PLAYED A HUGE ROLE in my life. I went to church on Sunday, attended religious instructions once a week, received all of my sacraments, and at the age of eight began the ritual of going to confession to ask God to forgive my sins. In my family we were also required to recite a prayer of thanks for the food that was put in front of us before every meal, and pray for the protection of the people we loved before going to bed.

But for me, bedtime prayers also came with the knowledge that I was never going to get into heaven.

I was going to hell.

In addition to praying for all the people I loved, what only God and I knew was that by the age of eight I was also praying for death. I wasn't praying for my own death. Yet. But for the death of someone I should've asked God to protect.

Why on earth would an eight-year-old pray for someone to die? Because in my confused and frightened mind, I only had two choices: reveal something that would break the heart of the person I loved more than anyone else in the world, or pray for the death of the person who was causing the confusion I was still too young to put into words.

If somehow this person had an accident or was kidnapped never to be seen again, then I wouldn't have to reveal something that would be the cause of everyone's pain, *and* I might have a better chance of getting into heaven, right?

Wrong.

Even I knew just hoping someone would die was breaking one of God's commandments. Although I prayed out loud for that person's safety, God could see what was in my heart.

My heart wasn't good.

My heart was black.

By the age of eight, I was already a very bad girl.

CHAPTER 1

She Is . . . Numb

"If you think you've had too much . . . hang on."
"Everybody Hurts" by R.E.M

THREE MONTHS AGO I WOKE UP IN SILENCE.

The alarm went off at the same time it did every morning, the dog licked my face, I sat up in bed, heard cars pulling out of driveways and the garbage truck rumbling down the street. I was aware of my surroundings, but internally there was only silence. My body's internal volume button broke. I called my ex-husband because the man I lived with—CJ, the man who swore he could never live without me—claimed he had no time for my "f'ing drama" as he left for work.

"I'm sick, Mike. My body won't stop shaking. My head won't stop shaking. I need you to get me to the ER." After sixteen years of marriage, Mike and I amicably separated several years before, but I always knew I could call him when in need.

I met Mike right before my twenty-sixth birthday when we were introduced by my cousin and his sister. Six months later we were engaged. For a long time I was dumbfounded that a man like Mike wanted to marry someone like me. Almost nine years older, he had been in the Navy, was married and divorced, owned a home, and was successful in his career. A year after our engagement we were married and when we returned from our honeymoon we began trying to get pregnant. After a miscarriage and eighteen months of marriage, our daughter, Kayla Rose, was born.

Once we settled into married life, it quickly became very clear how incompatible we actually were. Our outlooks on life differed, we had different interests, and as time went on our biggest connection was Kayla, who we centered our lives around. We created what looked like a solid, happy family life, but as a couple we struggled. And, the more we struggled the harder I was on myself.

I'd married a good man; a man who worked hard, looked after his family, was faithful, and was a good father. What more could a woman want? Why didn't I appreciate that this man chose me? Why couldn't I be happy? After fifteen years of marriage, we sat on the edge of our bed—a bed we hadn't slept in together for five years—and agreed we wanted each other to have a chance to find happiness and love with someone else.

The loneliness I felt and kept at bay, especially the last five years Mike and I were together, led me right to CJ. I was running so fast from my marriage that I jumped blindly into an eight year relationship. It began as an irresistible smolder and slowly grew into a raging, out of control fire that would come close to sucking the air from my lungs and suffocating me to death.

Half an hour after picking up the phone, Mike arrived and took me to the ER. For the first time in what seemed like forever, I finally took a deep breath.

After four hours of poking, prodding, and a CAT scan, I was proclaimed medically healthy. How could that be? The doctors could see my head shaking, my hands shaking, and my blood pressure was elevated. How could they send me home? I was sitting on a chair at the end of a hall waiting for Mike, who'd momentarily stepped away, when a woman who had first walked past doubled back and stopped in front of me.

"Are you okay?" Her voice was gentle and kind, and I noticed the hospital lanyard hanging from her neck.

"No, I'm not. I mean, the doctors have told me I am, but I know something is wrong . . ." My voice trailed off as a tear rolled down my cheek, and she pulled up a chair to sit next to me. She handed me a tissue.

"Are you comfortable talking to me about what's going on?" We sat there, off by ourselves, with tears slowly streaming down my face and her holding my hand as I told her how I woke up that morning numb, silent, and shaking. As she quietly prodded, it was a relief to have someone willing to listen to my concerns. I didn't even notice when Mike returned. I looked up when she asked if I would give her a few minutes to look into a couple of things and saw he was sitting across the hall.

When I introduced them, she asked me if it was okay to ask him a few questions. They shook hands and walked off together toward the elevator, quietly talking for several minutes. Mike came back, sat beside me, and we waited another fifteen minutes before she returned.

"Maureen, I have some good news. I can get you admitted." She stood in front of me, papers in hand. Immediately, a sense of relief and gratitude washed over me. She had listened! She heard me and was able to get the hospital to take me seriously. "I can get you a bed on the unit in about an hour, but we can start the paperwork right now."

For a moment, I felt relieved. But there was something about what she'd said that made me uncomfortable and the feeling of relief quickly disappeared.

"The unit? What unit?" I looked at her, then over at Mike, and I knew immediately what she meant. Many years ago I worked in an ER as a patient access representative. It was my responsibility to see the patients when they were finally brought back to an examination room, gather their information for the charts, and get them in the system. I understood exactly which unit had that empty bed.

"You want to put me in the psych unit?" My heart dropped. *No! I'm not being admitted to the psych unit.* "I'm not crazy! I thought you understood." Did Mike know what was happening? I felt betrayed. I wanted to scream but no sound, no words, no fight was in me. Instead, more silent tears stained my cheeks.

The woman sat beside me again, and, as I looked up, I could feel the compassion in her eyes. "If that is truly how you feel, there is another way I can help you." She handed me a piece of paper with a name and number on it. "I contacted a place called Forward Moving and was able to get you an intake interview tomorrow morning. You can attend on an outpatient basis. Call them for their address and speak with Delaney. These are the only two options I can give you."

This was what it had come to. The psych unit or an intensive outpatient program? My beautiful, intelligent, healthy daughter was coming home from college in less than a week. How could I allow her to come home to her mother in a psych unit? How would I possibly be able to explain that? Even making the choice to be in an outpatient program had me agonizing over what I would say to her.

I looked at the woman's badge. Her name was Annmarie. "Please, Annmarie. I'm not crazy . . ." I glanced over at Mike, then back at her.

I wished she could see me for who I once was—the me before that morning. I was the friend everyone came to when they needed advice and comfort, even as a teenager. And, when I wasn't listening and passing out hugs and advice, I was the friend making them roar with laughter. I was the woman who threw big birthday parties, holiday parties, team parties, and summer barbecues. I was the PTO President, and the mom who sat in the stands cheering her daughter on at softball games and during the high school halftime show as she performed with the marching band. I was the mom that took her daughter to concerts, sang with her at the top of our lungs on car rides, and surprised her husband with a trip to Alaska for his 50th birthday. I was the first woman in my family who was going to be happily married—the one who did it all the right way. That was me. Instead, the words I wanted to speak remained stuck in my throat, unable to be spoken.

"No, Maureen, you're not crazy," she assured me. "Please trust me. There are people who can help you get better. Promise me you will keep the appointment." I stared down at the paper in my hand and promised.

On the car ride home, I asked Mike if he would drive me to my appointment in the morning. "I don't want to tell CJ yet. He'll just make fun of me." Mike grabbed my hand as I started to cry. I asked him not to come before 8:15 the next morning.

CJ was usually gone by 8:00 a.m., but I wanted a fifteen-minute window in case he ran late.

At 8:30 a.m., Mike pulled up to my house with a cup of tea and a reassuring smile.

"How'd it go last night?" he asked as he handed me my tea.

"He didn't ask me anything. Just told me if I was home, it meant he was obviously right, and I was the Academy Award-winning drama queen he always knew I was." I took a sip and stared out the window.

"This is a good thing, Maureen. It's all going to be okay," he reassured me as he squeezed my hand. It struck me as ironic that as our marriage came to an end, all I wanted to do was run away from him and start a new life. Right now, sitting there in the car with him, it was the only place I felt safe. As we pulled up to the clinic, Mike promised to be back to pick me up at 4:00 p.m.

When I first walked in, Delaney was waiting by the front desk. She took me into her office and had me fill out a questionnaire. We talked about the day before and she explained how an intensive outpatient program was run. I would come on a daily basis from 11:00 a.m. to 4:00 p.m. for a variety of group therapy sessions. As I progressed, I would begin to step down to four days, then three days, then two days, until I was at one day a week, right before I graduated the program.

"This is the right place for you, Maureen. If you work the program, we can help you find your way back to good health."

She was so positive, so confident. As for me, I was still numb. "I'm going to bring you back to the waiting room. Your clinician will meet you momentarily and get you started."

Does everyone feel the way I do right now when they sit in this chair?

I'd never felt so lonely. I had no idea what to expect or what we would even discuss. I knew we'd be discussing my course of treatment and medication, but beyond that . . . Here I was, forty-nine-years-old, at the most desperate and vulnerable point in my life, waiting for doctors and clinicians I'd never met to call me in and explain everything I needed to know about my illness.

How do others take in the information hurled at them all at once?

I sat there wondering how the person responsible for explaining all the facts and information about what was happening to me understood the weight I carried on my chest? Did they know the anguish and confusion I felt? Would they understand that, right at that very moment, I couldn't fathom ever coming out the other end well and whole? Had they been through this? Or were they going to tell me what they know can, and probably will, happen to me physically and emotionally only because they've seen it happen to so many others who came before me?

The guilt and sadness suddenly hit me like water from a fire hose. I was slipping, falling, tumbling, and I couldn't catch my breath. My anxiety was so high, all I heard was thumping in my ears. I couldn't feel my head. It was pins and needles numb. The old Maureen would have picked her big girl panties up, jumped in a taxi, and driven as far away as possible from that place. The old Maureen would have dug her heels in and put up a battle. But, that Maureen was gone. The Maureen that sat there was void of any emotion or feeling other than fear. That Maureen had no fight left in her.

"Maureen Spataro?"

A friendly looking woman stood in front of me. I was looking at her, but for a few seconds I didn't see her. I was so far detached from what was going on anywhere other than in my head that all I could manage to do was look up with a blank, hollow stare.

"Are you Maureen?"

I nodded and managed a smile.

"Hi Maureen, I'm Tessa. I have to tell you right off the bat that I'm already impressed, because not only did you show up, you're early! I'm going to take you on back, and I'll give you a tour of our facility."

Tessa started off by reiterating how the IOP works. From start to finish, it was a three-month program. "I know at first this is going to be overwhelming. That's completely normal and understandable."

Normal? I wanted to grab Tessa by her shoulders and shout

through gritted teeth, "There is nothing normal about any of this! Everything I'm about to do for the next three months was never supposed to be part of my life. None of this was supposed to happen to me. I want to know why. WHY? How could my life come to this? Everything I tried to sidestep, avoid, find better ways for—it was all for nothing. I did it all wrong and now I'm here. I don't give a shit if every patient has felt exactly the way I do; I'm the one walking through this door. Normal is the last word I would use to describe every scenario, every fear, and every ounce of anxiety running through my mind and body at this very moment." Instead, I walked next to her as we toured the clinic—silent, terrified, and keenly aware of the shame that enveloped me.

"On the left are our administration offices. Up here on the right are the treatment rooms. The building is divided into two areas: adults and adolescents. This is where the adult treatment rooms are and this room right here is where you'll be. Why don't you take a seat? Harper will be in shortly to get things started."

Yellow walls. Blue chairs. Paintings of beach cottages along a shoreline. I guess that was considered soothing for a treatment room. Perhaps one day I would feel comforted, but for now, all I could think was that this couldn't be my life. I didn't want to meet Harper.

Oh God, please . . . please . . . I can't face any of this. I simply won't live through these treatments. If I have to do this, I will die. I don't have the strength to get through. Please, God, please make this stop! Please don't . . .

I shut my eyes because I didn't want the tears to start, but it was too late. All I could hope for now was that I could quiet the sobs as I completely broke down. An avalanche of thoughts and questions invaded my mind. But the one question that never left: would I ever be able to find my way back to my life?

"Here you go."

I felt something on my lap, opened my eyes, and saw that there were six other people assembled in the room with me and one of them had placed a box of tissues on my lap. I smiled gratefully, dabbed my eyes, and took a deep breath.

And so it began.

Welcome to my nervous breakdown.

CHAPTER 2

She Is . . . Lost

"Mental wounds still screaming, driving me insane . . ."
"Crazy Train" by Ozzy Osborn

"GOOD MORNING, EVERYONE." A YOUNG woman walked in and doubt immediately sank in. This was Harper? She was young enough to be my daughter. This was the person who was going to help me? What on earth could this child possibly say or show me that I hadn't already heard or tried? My hopelessness shot to DEFCON 4.

"Before we begin, I'd like to welcome our new member, Maureen. To make Maureen feel more welcome, let's go around the room, give your name, state the reason you're here, and give one random fact about yourself."

I despised this. Why hadn't introducing yourself to a room filled with strangers become outlawed? Did I look like I wanted to hear about anyone else's issues? I barely got myself out of bed, showered, and brushed my teeth. I was going deaf from the chaos that had seemingly taken up residence in my mind. What on earth gave Harper the impression I wanted someone else's chaos stopping in for a chat?

The first person to introduce himself was Sean. He was about my age, with very dark eyes, a pointed, goateed chin, and very well-spoken. He chose his words carefully and deliberately. "My name is Sean I'm here for anxiety, depression, and suicide ideation. A random fact about me is that I am a school principal."

What did he just say? Did he just say suicide ideation? What the hell was ideation? Does ideation mean he had already attempted suicide or he was just thinking about it? I hadn't thought about or attempted suicide. Someone put me in the wrong group. I could hear my heart beating in my ears and feel my body tensing up. I wanted to stand up and say to Harper, "I'm sorry, but there's been a mistake. I don't belong here. I'm not this sick." Instead, I sat in my fear, my mind racing out of control as another introduction began.

"My name is Marilyn." Marilyn sat next to Sean. She was around my age, slender, black hair, dressed stylishly, and couldn't sit still. "I'm also here for anxiety, depression, attempted suicide, and suicide ideation. A random fact about me is that I am a lawyer."

A school principal and a lawyer, both with suicide ideation?

I was momentarily snapped out of my own fear by two random thoughts: if I saw them standing in line at an airport or supermarket, I would never in a million years think they were so troubled, and perhaps I should stop beating myself up for not being someone "more important," like a principal or lawyer.

I was brought back to what was going on in the room by the voice of a beautiful eighteen-year-old girl with porcelain skin, flawless makeup, and bright purple hair. Her clothing and overall persona screamed fashionista, and I briefly smiled.

"Hi! My name is Jenna. I'm here for anxiety, depression, bipolar disorder, borderline personality disorder, and self-harm. A random fact about me is that I have an older brother and a younger sister."

Self-harm? She hurts herself? The urge to flee or insist I be put in the correct group was almost uncontrollable. Suicide, cutting, mental disorders I'd never heard of . . . I was not one of "those" people. I was stronger than this. I was better than this, right?

"My name is Jackson. I'm here for psychosis and depression." Jackson was twenty-two years old and arguably the sweetest looking young man I had ever laid eyes upon. The rich, deep tone in his voice didn't match the innocence of his face, but I imagined his shy smile and deep brown eyes melted the hearts of most of the young girls he met. "A random fact about me is that I play the guitar."

"May I ask again, because my memory is so bad, what exactly is psychosis?" Marilyn's leg shook at the speed of a thoroughbred running in the Kentucky Derby as she spoke up.

"That's a great question, Marilyn, and we'll be learning all about the various mental illnesses each of you suffers from during our education sessions. Without getting too in-depth, in the simplest terms, psychosis is when you have lost all sense of reality." Before I could react to what Harper just said, Marilyn asked another question.

"Am I allowed to ask how someone gets psychosis?" She turned to Jackson. He nodded gently and smiled.

"In my case, drugs," he told her. "Drugs caused me to lose all sense of reality. I started seeing things that weren't there, hearing voices and things that weren't real, and lost all sense of what was really going on around me."

Listening to Jackson explain how he developed his mental illness drew me in, and for the first time, I was out of my own head. Looking at him, how at ease he seemed to be talking about what brought him here, was compelling. Here was a young man who was a seemingly "normal" boy, living a "normal" life, who experimented in a way many young people did, but reacted in a way most do not.

My heart stopped pounding and I took a deep breath. But that was only temporary. Within minutes, my mind raced back to something Harper said, something about educating us on the various mental illnesses that brought us here. When would I be permitted to let her know I did not suffer from a mental illness? When would she stop including me in this group?

I AM NOT ONE OF THESE PEOPLE!

My growing anxiety attack was interrupted by Ted introducing himself. "My name is Ted and I'm here for anxiety, depression, suicide ideation, and PTSD. A random fact about me is that I am an artist. I paint." He was very tall, very fidgety, and bug-eyed.

"Okay, Maureen," I heard Harper say. "Introduce yourself to the group, tell them why you're here, and give one random fact about yourself."

My inner voice was screaming "NO!" but I looked over at Sean and the expression on his face was oddly reassuring, like he was telling me, "Just say it. It's okay. We get it."

"My name is Maureen. I'm here for anxiety, depression, and PTSD." *At least that's what I've been told.* I wanted to ask if anyone noticed that I hadn't mentioned a mental illness such as suicide ideation, bipolar disorder, psychosis, or borderline personality disorder, but I controlled the impulse. "A random fact about me is that I lived in Houston, Texas for two years."

I hadn't thought about Houston for quite some time. I actually stayed eighteen months longer than I should have. I ran away from home after meeting a handsome cowboy on a trip to Mexico when I was nineteen. We got engaged six months after meeting, but my parents wouldn't let me move to Texas without the wedding ring, so I just got up one day and took off.

In hindsight, taking off to "live in sin" with my cowboy instead of marrying him was one of the best decisions I ever made, because two years later I was on a plane headed back to New York. My cowboy had become an everyday beer-drinking, DUI-collecting, speed-snorting shell of the beautiful boy I met, and I had grown weary of the party life after the first six months.

"Thank you, Maureen, and welcome. Can we go over the rules for Maureen?" Our chairs were in a semi-circle and Harper was at the helm.

"What happens in this room stays in this room." Jenna was the first to pipe in. "We do not discuss what is said during processing to anyone. We don't talk about it in the halls or lunchroom with other patients, or other group members, or with anyone outside of this building."

Processing? What does that mean? Patients? This isn't a hospital; I am not a patient.

"No judgments." Ted explained that our group and the room we were in was a non-judgment area. "We don't form opinions or pass judgment on any group member." Too late. I'd already broken that rule, because the first thought that crossed my mind when I laid eyes on Ted was that he was definitely the group member most likely to go postal. "No cross-talking." Jackson explained that when a group member was processing, no one was permitted to have a "side bar" conversation with another group member. We were not allowed to interrupt a group member when they were speaking.

"We don't give advice," Marilyn chimed in. "We can share similar experiences and how we may have dealt with it, or how we feel about what they are saying, but we cannot give advice or tell them what we think they should do."

Wasn't the point of the group to give guidance and advice? Weren't our clinicians supposed to be telling us, "advising" us, about how to handle our problems and illnesses? If not, then what the hell was I doing here? Were we all just here to tell stories, hug it out, and sing Kumbaya at the end of each session? Someone still hadn't told me how I got here.

"Maureen, I'm not going to push you to process with the group today. If you feel like you have something to share, by all means share it. But we usually give new members a few days to get a feel of how everything is done and get used to the daily routines before trying to coax them into opening up."

I nodded to let Harper know I understood. I was already exhausted, frightened, confused, and numb. I had to figure out a way to get my heart to stop pounding in my chest and accept that the next couple of days were going to be filled with phrases and routines completely foreign to me. But I was relieved to finally find out that processing meant talking and sharing with the group.

"Okay. Let's go around the room and take our pulse before we get into processing," Harper said.

Pulse was a series of questions everyone must answer: name, clinician's name, did you see the doctor this week, did you have a family session, are you taking your meds, two words to describe how you're feeling, appetite, sleep, and so on. It gave the clinician running your processing session an idea of where you were emotionally. Although I was exempt from processing, I was not exempt from pulse. Everyone in the room went through their individual pulse and Harper looked at me.

My name is Maureen and my clinician is Tessa. Since today is only my first day, I haven't met with the doctor here, so there are no medication changes. I am compliant with what I've been prescribed by my medical doctor. I have no suicidal thoughts or thoughts of self-harm. Two feelings are . . . I couldn't say anything. My lips turned down hard into a pout and the tears welled up in my eyes.

"It's okay, Maureen. Take a deep breath and take your time." I thought about my daughter, my family, my friends, and how fearful I was that there was a real possibility the person they know and loved was gone forever. Would they all be better off without me here?

The Maureen who sat there was a girl no one but me knew. She was so frightening that I'd pushed her away my whole life.

She was weak and undeserving. She could also be angry and violent.

"Two feelings are numb and shame."

Maureen was never supposed to be born. All the hopes and dreams her mother had were lost because of her.

"I haven't had a family session."

A disappointment as a daughter, a failure as a mother and wife. She is ugly, fat, and stupid.

"My appetite is non-existent."

She's come close to surfacing over the years, but I always find a way to calm her down and put her to rest.

"I haven't slept in six days."

This time, I couldn't get a hold of her. Somehow she escaped me and managed to unravel my life in less than three months.

I heard my voice, but it was the voice inside of me that I wished Harper could hear.

Please help me. I'm literally dying. Please, I'm begging you. Don't make me work through this. I don't think I'll survive.

CHAPTER 3

She Is . . . Blind

"Do you feel better now, as she falls to the ground?"
"Face Down" by Red Jumpsuit Apparatus

"OKAY EVERYONE, WHO IS GOING TO PRO-
cess?" Harper said as I glanced around the room. Everyone was
either staring at the floor or off into space. "Those of you who
have been here for a while know how this works. Someone takes
the floor or I choose."

After a moment, Ted spoke up, but I couldn't focus on
what he was saying. I was still trying to get a hold of my own
thoughts, and I was losing the battle. I was exhausted from lack
of sleep. Ted discussed his job and how his boss was out to get
him.

I felt nothing; no sympathy, no empathy, no sadness, no
compassion, no urge to say something witty to make him smile.

The empathetic woman who was never at a loss for some words of comfort, a reassuring smile, or a tight hug no longer occupied this body. In her place was an endless, empty void in which no light or emotions were capable of existing.

As Ted continued to describe how he drove his car into a cement divider on a bridge, I didn't even glance up. I didn't care what brought him here. I didn't care what brought anyone here to this room. Ted made me nervous as he spoke, his voice just one decibel shy of shouting. My anxiety started to rise and my discomfort grew. Sitting in the middle of this room was similar to sitting in a room with CJ. I was on guard about what he would say—worried that just one innocent comment would lead to an argument or worse.

I met CJ almost five years ago, when my marriage was ending. He was well over 6'5", retired, and from the start I wholeheartedly believed he was the love of my life. We seemed to have everything in common, and I felt like I could be myself when I was with him. We loved to sing at the top of our lungs to our favorite songs on the radio and talk nonstop into the early morning. Every red light was an excuse for him to lean over in the car to plant a kiss on my lips. He told me he loved me on our fourth date. I fell hard and fast. He made me feel beautiful and sexy, and he got a kick out of me. Within five months, we, along with my daughter Kayla, were living together.

By the end of the second month, I started to see subtle

flashes of impatience. At first, it was little things: I didn't put the toilet paper on the holder the right way. I loaded the dishwasher incorrectly. I ate "his" cookies. Instead of questioning him, I told myself they weren't battles worth fighting. I made sure I hung the toilet paper the right way, loaded the dishwasher the way he preferred, and didn't take anything until I made sure it wasn't a special treat he bought for himself. I simply wanted to be happy and continue to make him happy, and none of the issues he had were so important that I couldn't adjust.

What I didn't know was how quickly small issues were going to mushroom into life-altering problems. Ironically, Kayla was the first person to see CJ for who he really was and it would change the course of our lives for years to come.

The three of us were in CJ's car, coming home from dinner one night, and we were joking around, giving each other a hard time. I don't recall what I said, but it was in response to a wisecrack CJ made. Kayla and I dissolved into giggles. CJ was holding my hand as he always did, but as we giggled, he yanked it toward him and squeezed it hard enough that I instinctively tried to pull it back. He was laughing, too, but his grip was solid and I couldn't get my hand free.

"What the fuck was that? Don't you grab her like that." Kayla was sixteen and sitting in the back of the car. I turned around in shock and faced her.

35

"What did you just say? Apologize right this second!" I was so angry. Why would she speak that way?

"No! He shouldn't grab you that way. Daddy never grabbed you like that. Who the hell does he think he is?" She was holding her ground and refused to back down.

"Kayla! You *will* apologize right this second." I was mortified that she would curse so unapologetically and speak so disrespectfully. Kayla was always her own person, even as a child, but this behavior was beyond that and completely out of character.

Kayla continued to refuse to apologize to CJ and we argued the rest of the weekend. You could cut the tension in our house with a knife. When it came to a head, I told her if she wasn't going to apologize and didn't like the rules in our home, she could move back with her father.

Until the day I die, I will regret those words; regret not taking a breath before giving the person I loved the most in this entire world that ultimatum. Within an hour, she packed herself up and had me drive her "home." I told myself that once she calmed down, she'd come back to live with me. Eventually, she and CJ made peace, but we would never again live under the same roof. She chose to divide her time between home with her father and my house. Home was no longer with me. I cried almost every night for six months.

Once Kayla left, the relationship between CJ and me shifted and the things he loved about me became the things he slowly began to criticize. He blurted out one day that he hated my hair straight, so I started wearing it curly. Another time, when I went to kiss him good-bye, he turned his head with a disgusted look on his face. "I *hate* kissing a woman who wears lipstick." When I asked him how long he'd felt that way, he said, "Always," but didn't want to deal with the drama.

"What drama? Because you don't like lipstick?" I didn't understand.

"*This* drama, Maureen. I tell you I don't like something and you gotta push for a why." Did he think I was questioning why he didn't like lipstick? What was I missing?

"I'm not pushing for a reason why you don't like lipstick. I just feel bad you thought I would be upset with you. If I had known, I simply would have said okay and stopped wearing it." Was I difficult to talk to?

"But instead you're going to beat the subject to death and nag the shit out of me like you are right now. You love drama, Maureen. Just say okay and stop wearing lipstick. That's all you have to do. If you just listened to me, there wouldn't be a problem." I didn't love drama. I avoided it at all costs. I wished I knew why he felt that way.

I stopped wearing lipstick.

Then there was the night I came home after picking up some new clothes. CJ asked me to show him what I bought. When I came out in the new pants I loved, CJ tilted his head, grinned, and said, "You know I love a woman with curves, but you need to cut back on the dessert. Your ass looks pregnant." He laughed at himself, repeating the punchline. When I didn't laugh back, he became annoyed and accused me of being too sensitive and not having a sense of humor. I was the same size and weight as when we met, but it didn't matter. In my mind, I was fat and unattractive.

I started doing everything I could to "fix" the things that upset CJ. The more unhappy he seemed, the harder I tried to be funnier, prettier, sexier, a better woman. Nothing I did would ever make him happy and the stakes continued to get higher.

The first time CJ hit me, we were on a trip. I promised Kayla I would call her to let her know we got there safely, but I left my phone in our room. CJ, who never let anyone touch his phone, dialed Kayla's number and handed it to me so I could reassure her we were there. We were at the beach bar and a guy struck up a conversation with CJ, so I walked a few feet away to talk.

As I tried to figure out which button to hit to hang up, a topless picture of a friend of ours popped up on the screen. Below it, she had written, "How do you like my tan lines, baby?" He wrote back to her, "I love them and I love you SOOOO much, baby. I'll call you later."

It felt like all the blood drained from my body. I couldn't believe what I was looking at, what I was reading. My mind immediately jumped to the drive to the resort. About halfway through our trip, CJ asked if I could drive because he was getting a headache. Apparently, as I'd played chauffeur, CJ soothed his headache by sexting with his other girlfriend – a woman I knew.

I stood frozen as I stared at the blonde, curly-haired woman who had been to my house with her husband on several occasions and with whom CJ and I double dated. I couldn't decide if I wanted to smash his phone into the ground or stick it in his face. I decided on the latter and when I brought the phone back to show him what popped up, I told him he could cab it back to Jersey.

I raced back to our room ahead of him, knowing he had to pay the drink bill, and repacked the clothes I had unpacked just an hour before. I felt like a fool. I surprised him with a "romantic" weekend in this sweet, lazy beach town in Massachusetts, but his mind and apparently his dick was thinking about another woman in New Jersey. My hands were shaking, my heart was thumping, and all I wanted to do was run as far away from where we were as quickly as possible. As I grabbed my pocketbook and the car keys, CJ stormed into the room.

"What the fuck are you doing, Maureen?" He stood in front of the door. "Are you crazy?"

"How do you like her tan lines, CJ? You love her so much?" Although I managed to stay calm, I couldn't hold back the tears.

"I'm going back to Jersey. Let her know you have an empty bed for two nights. I'd ask you why, but it doesn't matter." I knew something was up. I even asked him if he was cheating, but he denied it and told me I was being silly. Deny, deny, deny . . . the cheater's creed.

"You're crazy! She sent that text to me by mistake. It was for her husband Craig and she sent it to me by mistake. I was joking when I responded. What the fuck is the matter with you?" Did he actually think I was going to believe him?

"Get away from the door, CJ. Do you think I'm a fool? You're screwing her and now you're going to try to lie to me?" I walked toward him and tried to move him away from the door with my hip, but he wouldn't budge.

"You're not going anywhere. Give me my car keys," he demanded. "You're fucking crazy! You don't think I'm going to let you drive off in *my* car, do you?" He was actually grinning.

"Get out of my way, CJ." When I approached him this time, I planted my feet and pushed my hip into him harder. For a second, he lost his balance and I was able to open the door. As I took the first step to walk out, he grabbed me, pulled me back into the room, slammed the door, and shoved me with both hands over the bed. I bounced off the other side and hit my head on the wall. Before I could get to my feet, he was standing over me, grabbing me by the front of my shirt, and lifting me off the ground. The back collar of my shirt was slowly digging into my neck.

"You c**t!" He threw me to the other side of the room and smacked me across the head. "You're not going anywhere! You even try to take my car, I'll call the police and have you arrested. Stupid bitch! Don't you ever put your hands on me again!"

He sat me down and "explained" that Michelle was sexting with her husband and simply sent it to him by mistake because CJ came right before Craig in her phone directory. I wanted to point out to him that their daughter Courtney, and two sons Craig, Jr. and Connor would have probably come before Craig, but after his reaction I was afraid things would escalate again.

Apology after apology. Endless begging. That's what I got the first time he hit me. He swore up and down he'd never cheat on me; he loved me too much. He told me I was being paranoid and that I was his one and only.

I stayed.

The next time he hit me, the apology and promises were followed with, "You know how I get when I think you're going to leave me. I love you! If you would just listen to me, everything would be okay."

We fought after our Halloween party. When I tried to leave the room, he grabbed me from behind. I reached up to push him away and ended up scratching his face by mistake. He yelled out and threw me down the hallway, and as I got to my feet, he caught up to me and kicked me down the staircase. He picked me up from the bottom of the steps and slapped me as hard as he could across my ear and face. He quite literally slapped the spit out of me.

The third time he hit me, I stopped believing the apologies and packed my bags. He grabbed our dog by the neck and shook her like a rag doll. He only stopped when I unpacked and promised not to leave.

The fourth time he hit me, I left and went to my brother's house. CJ broke in when I was home alone one afternoon and put a gun to my head. "If you don't come back, I'll kill everyone you love and then kill myself. I'll leave you alone so you can always remember what you did."

I went back.

"Maureen? Maureen?" I quickly opened my eyes and turned as I heard Sean's voice. I'd dozed off and our group was breaking up.

"I'm sorry. I . . . I just haven't slept in days." I was a little confused and stammering.

"It happens to all of us, especially early on. You'll eventually be able to sleep and the naps won't be an issue." Sean quickly patted my shoulder as he walked out of the room.

I looked up at Harper and apologized.

"Sean is right. We'll get you sleeping regularly again. Right now, we're just glad you're here," she told me.

I smiled thankfully at Harper and packed up to head home. As I passed Tessa's office, she popped her head out, calling me back.

"So, you made it through the first day." Tessa was a woman with wildly untamed black hair, a Demi Moore-type voice, big brown eyes, and a wide, toothy smile. "I'm not going to ask anything of you this first week except to just show up. You may wake up and feel like you just can't, but do it anyway, okay?"

"I will. I promise I will come back. I made a promise to my family that I would do whatever you tell me to do, and I will keep that promise. I will see you tomorrow morning." The tone in my voice was void of any emotion.

"If those are your reasons for getting out of bed and coming back again tomorrow, I'll take it. My goal is to get you to the point that you are working through the program for yourself. For now, particularly the first week, whatever gets you up and back to us is what I'll ask you to use as your motivation. You can't see it right now and I know you don't feel it, but you can do this, Maureen. You are a warrior with a fragile soul. There is remarkable strength within you. It's what brought you through your life." I desperately wanted to feel the way Tessa did. She was so passionate and believed every word she said.

"So, how did it go?" Mike was waiting for me, just as he'd promised. "If you don't want to talk about it, that's okay. I just wanted to make sure you were comfortable." I explained how the day ran and was touched by his concern.

Mike was a good man; he always had been. And he was a great father to Kayla. Nothing terrible ended our marriage. We just grew apart. At least that was how I chose to sum it up. There was no cheating, no abuse, no drama. We both just checked out, me being the one who checked out first.

As we drove, I thought about Tessa's words: "There is a fighter within you. You are a warrior with a fragile soul." The only word I could relate to at the moment was *fragile*. A warrior? A fighter in me? I had no more fight left. I would always be a woman whose mere presence destroyed lives and brought nothing but shame, resentment, sadness, and a constant reminder of what could have been to those who loved her.

The only success I could claim was that I gave birth to a magnificent young woman. But even that was marred by the fact that the strong, independent, confident survivor she believed her mother to be was actually a weak, frightened failure who couldn't even wrap her mind around the simplest thought. I was as much of a weight on my daughter's back as I was around my mother's waist.

Mike's voice snapped me back to the moment. "So, what are you going to tell CJ?" I dreaded telling CJ. I had to go out on medical disability for three months. He didn't even like when I took a day off unless, of course, it was because he needed me to take a day off to go somewhere with him or take him to the doctor. I knew I couldn't successfully complete this program living in the same house together. I already knew I was going to leave.

"The truth. I'm going to tell him the truth. Whatever the fallout, I am going to complete this program, Mike." I didn't tell CJ that I'd called Mike to take me to the ER. I'd made it home before he got back from work. He never asked how I was feeling, only if I was going to work today. When I told him I had a doctor's appointment, he walked toward the living room muttering, "Such a drama queen" and telling me I better not get fired. I spent the rest of the night watching TV in our bedroom.

As we pulled up in front of my house, Mike squeezed my hand. "You need anything, just call." He knew things weren't good between CJ and me. He didn't know the entire story—no one really did—but he knew there were issues. I hugged him tightly. This was a side of Mike I never saw when we were married. He was always so stoic, so unemotional.

"Just promise me you won't say anything to Kayla," I pleaded. "We'll tell her everything when she comes home for winter break." Mike promised. "Thank you for doing this for me." I hugged him again and stepped out of the car. As I did, my front door opened and CJ stood there. He waved to Mike, smiling like it was just another day. But I knew what was coming.

"Hey . . ." Mike said to me. "Remember, if you need me

to come and get you in the morning, I'll be here." I smiled and faced the house. CJ had stepped away from the door. As I turned the knob and walked in, all I prayed was that he would simply be too annoyed to care why I was with Mike.

But I knew better.

CHAPTER 4

She Is . . . Desperate

"I just wanna live while I'm alive."
"It's My Life" by Bon Jovi

CJ WAS ALREADY SITTING IN HIS RECLINER AS I walked in the door.

"Hey." I closed the door as he ignored me, which was nothing new. I had a 50/50 chance, depending on what kind of mood he was in, of getting an acknowledgement. I walked straight to the bedroom and took off my shoes. I'd just turned on the TV and laid down when I heard him get up from his chair and walk down the hall. He stopped at the bedroom door.

"So what, now you have Mike taking you to your doctor's appointment? Were your head and hands shaking so bad you couldn't drive yourself?" CJ laughed at his own sarcasm. He was his own biggest fan. He sat on his side of the bed to put on his socks and sneakers. Tonight was bowling night. I loved bowling night because he didn't come home until after I was asleep. I could spend the night with our dog Lulu, simply relaxing and pretending I lived alone.

"He offered after taking me to the ER yesterday and wanted to make sure I actually kept my appointment." CJ wasn't jealous of Mike; he just couldn't stand anyone making him look bad.

"Ohhhh. You didn't tell me he took you to the ER yesterday. Guess you couldn't keep it a secret, huh? Always trying to keep things from me, Maureen. Always think you're smarter than you are. In the end, I always find out the truth. So did you talk shit about me? You'll do anything to make me look like an asshole, won't you? So what did the doctor say? What is it now, Maureen?"

"I didn't go to see a doctor today. I went to a facility in Freehold to start an intensive outpatient program. I have to go every day to participate in various group sessions with clinicians. I'm breaking down, CJ." I hated myself for it, but I started to cry. I was so lost. I just wanted him to be nice, to show he at least cared for me as a human being. He didn't even turn around.

"As I work through the program, I'll start going fewer days a week until I'm down to one and can graduate. In total, I will be out of work for three months." My heart was beating out of my chest. Could I be any more pathetic? I should've felt safe, I should've felt good about sharing this with the man who was supposed to love me, but instead I knew this was the last piece of information he needed to completely convince me I was a lunatic. He didn't disappoint.

"So let me get this straight. You're gonna take a three-month vacation to sit in a bunch of circles with other people who are as crazy as you are to talk about why you're so sad? You're a piece of work, Maureen. How the hell are we gonna be able to afford you being out of work for three months? You're gonna get fired."

"I'm not going to lose my job, CJ. I will go out on disability. That's what it's there for. It's called benefits for a reason." I was so tired of defending myself. So tired of being told I was crazy, bipolar, out of my mind, fat ass, ugly mole-face bitch, and the countless other degrading things he called me.

"This is such bullshit!" CJ stomped around the house, getting ready to go bowling. I was relieved because I wouldn't have to listen to his never-ending tirade of insults and badgering. "Now we'll have less money coming in because of you and your little breakdown. Perfect. Just perfect."

According to what he told me when we were looking for houses to rent early on, CJ cleared over $4,000 a month. I said according to him because I never saw a statement. CJ's entire life was locked up: phone, bank accounts, whereabouts, friends, and even family. As I sat listening to his tirade, I thought about all the things I didn't know about him. With my small salary, we should bring in almost $6,000 a month, but the way he spent money, we still never seemed to have enough. He was angry because he'd have less money to piss away, less money to ask me to front him until his check was deposited. He was still muttering as he angrily stomped out the front door and screeched away from the house.

I laid in bed and thought about everything that brought me to this point; all the mistakes I'd made and all the people I'd disappointed. As I buried myself in the endless loop of missteps, I wondered for a brief moment if I was one of "those people" in my group. Suicide ideation happens in the blink of an eye. You agonize over the realization that the only thing guaranteed is waking up every morning in pain, fear, and shame. When you wake up in silence, you have fallen to a level of hopelessness and exhaustion for which there is no end, and your heart, your mind, and your soul dies off.

But in the next second, my reason for showing up every day and completing this program came into focus. My Kayla. I thought about the day she was born. The nurse brought her into my room after everyone left for our first official mother/daughter "girl time." I had an emergency C-section that morning and wasn't awake when she was born. I drifted in and out of sleep the entire day and that moment was the first time I had her all to myself. She was so quiet and content laying there, just staring at my face as I unwrapped her. I looked at her tiny fingers and toes and covered her in hundreds of kisses. I couldn't believe how beautiful she was, so perfect in every way. I was overcome with a love I didn't know was possible until then.

As I recalled that night, I realized that there was no pain so great that I would willingly prevent myself from ever seeing my daughter's face, hearing her laughter, or telling her how much I loved her. On my worst day, she remained the person who brought me my greatest joy. I would always love her more than life itself.

CHAPTER 5

She Is . . . Ready to Escape

"The road is calling, today is the day."
"Don't Look Back" by Boston

FOR THE NEXT TWO DAYS, JUST GETTING OUT of bed was not only emotionally painful, but physically painful, as well. I woke up each morning quietly crying, feeling an excruciating loneliness that pinned me to the mattress simply by its weight. CJ left early for his part-time job, and it was a relief not to have to tiptoe around him or hold my breath as I anticipated a nasty comment.

I left for the facility at 10:30 a.m. The clinicians kept their promise and didn't call upon me. I followed the crowd to learn the routine and sat in the break room alone during our lunch break. My appetite was nonexistent and the internal loneliness never subsided.

I couldn't imagine ever feeling whole again. When I arrived

home at 5:00 p.m., CJ barely spoke to me, and when he did, it was short and curt. I was hanging on by a thread and I knew leaving was my only option. I'd been down that road with him before and I knew he was just biding his time before the insults and putdowns started again, and my gut told me I wouldn't get through it. I had an excused absence because I had another scheduled appointment, but I'd already canceled it.

CJ's alarm rang and I listened as he went through his morning routine: shut alarm off, check phone, go to the bathroom (with phone), wash his face, brush his teeth, go into the kitchen to make coffee, come back to the bedroom and get dressed, pour a mug of coffee, grab his coat and hat, out the door. I listened as I heard the car motor get farther away before I got up.

I threw myself together and started packing my clothes, my pictures, and my Christmas ornaments. I knew I could only take the minimal amount of things, so I decided pictures and ornaments were the most important. Lulu watched me and my tears flowed. I couldn't take her. She was older and I was heading to my brother's house, where two other dogs already lived. I knew CJ would take care of her, but leaving her behind broke my heart. She'd been my comfort through all the bad times, but I knew if I took her it would be worse. In my heart, I knew she wouldn't adjust to the other dogs, so she had to stay behind.

Once I'd packed, I called my sister-in-law, Maryann. She and my brother Chris agreed to let me stay in their spare room.

"Do you have everything you're going to take?" she asked. They were hoping I would leave CJ for some time. Every time I left, it was their house where I went to stay.

"I have the necessities." I was suddenly scared that CJ would come home. I just wanted to go.

"You can't go back, Maureen. Whatever is packed is it, so just make sure . . ." I knew she was looking out for me, but I just needed her to come over and help me leave.

"I know, Mare. Come now." I hung up and started moving stuff down the steps. Lulu was laying at the top of the stairs and I started to cry again. I suddenly decided to get her stuff together: food bowl, leash, sweaters . . . and thought, "Fuck it, I'll make it work." But as I reevaluated what I was doing, I realized it was impossible for her to come with me and put everything on the kitchen table as my sister-in-law pulled up.

Maryann walked in the door and started grabbing the few things I had. "Is this it? Nothing else? You're sure?" I nodded and teared up quietly, looked back at my Lulu one last time and closed the door behind me. As we jumped quickly into our cars, I thought about the day I moved in with CJ.

I sat on the ledge of the big bay window looking out on the front lawn, giddily waiting for him to come home. Although my marriage had been a good one, there was no passion. We were two good people who built a nice life together, but weren't meant to be. And, before that I had been in volatile and abusive relationships in one form or another, going back to when I was a young girl. Meeting CJ felt like I finally met the man I was supposed to build the rest of my life with; the man with whom I had found love, safety, a partner, and my forever. As I waited for him, I silently thanked God. "This is my reward for everything I've been through. I will always be thankful to you, and I promise every day will be happier than the one before."

The pain in my chest was crushing as I began to sob at the memory. I could never have foreseen that the day which held so much joy and promise for the future would end with me throwing two suitcases of clothing, a bag of photos, and my Christmas ornaments in the back seat of my car, and running away.

After unpacking at my brother's house and settling in for a few hours, I was distracted from crying when my niece arrived home from school.

"Aunt Maureen! I knew you were here when I saw your car! Are you going to stay for dinner?" Emily was nine years old, and my first niece and only goddaughter. I simply adored her.

"Actually, Aunt Maureen is going to be staying with us for a while. She is going to sleep in the spare room." Maryann said it so matter-of-factly, I almost forgot the reason why, at the age of forty-nine, I was now living in my younger brother's house.

Emily looked back over to me and screamed, "You're *living* with us? YAAY!" She ran over to give me a huge hug. Then suddenly, as if it hit her, she asked the inevitable. "You're not living with CJ anymore?"

"No, doll. I'm not living with CJ anymore. Sometimes things just don't work out." Oh, please let that be a good enough answer.

"It's okay, you're living here now!" She was so happy, which put the first smile on my face all day. And when my other niece, Lily, and nephew, Sean, arrived, Emily was more than happy to let them know she had a new housemate. Hearing the three kids playing reminded me of when Kayla was their age and playdates were an everyday occurrence. But I was suddenly exhausted and let Maryann know I was going to lie down for a half hour. As I walked upstairs to my new room, the phone rang and she picked it up.

"No, you can't speak to her (pause). I'm sorry, but she's not coming to the phone (pause). Don't curse at me that way (pause). I'm hanging up now." Maryann went back to cooking when the phone rang again.

"She doesn't want to speak to you, CJ (pause). I would prefer if you didn't talk to me that way (pause). That's not a good idea (pause). Please do not show up here (pause). I'm hanging up now." This time, Maryann got the kids from the family room and instructed them to go up to Emily's room. As I stood on the stairs watching the kids go up to Emily's room, there was a banging on the door.

"MAUREEN! MAUREEN! TALK TO ME! MAUREEN!" He was banging so loudly, the dogs barked in unison and my body started to shake.

"What is that?" My nephew, Sean, heard CJ's voice. "Aunt Maureen, is that CJ? Why won't you talk to him? Are you mad at him?" Sean was nervous as he questioned me.

"Why don't you go to Emily's room, sweetie? Right now, CJ is just upset, but everything is okay." As I heard Sean's little footsteps continue up the stairs I slowly sat down on the step, leaning over with my elbows on my knees, hands tightly covering my mouth, too paralyzed to move.

"OPEN THIS FUCKING DOOR!" Oh God, I just knew he was going to break the door down. Just as that thought crossed my mind, I heard Maryann open it. In my head now, I was screaming, *NO! DON'T OPEN THE DOOR!*

"CJ, I have all the kids here and you are scaring them . . ."

"MAUREEN! TALK TO ME!" he shouted around her. "Tell her to come outside. I just want to talk to her." CJ pleaded, but I knew I couldn't go to him.

"CJ, Maureen is not going to come outside. She doesn't want to see you. The kids are here and you are making a scene. Please go home." Maryann was as cool as a cucumber.

"MAUREEN! I LOVE YOU! PLEASE DON'T DO THIS! PLEASE, MAUREEN!" *Oh God, make him stop.*

"I'm going back inside, CJ. Please go home." And with that,

I heard the door close No more bashing at the door, no more pleas. Just the screeching of CJ's wheels as he raced away.

Maryann locked the door behind her and came around to the bottom of the steps where I was sitting. She mouthed to me that everything would be okay, and called up to the kids that dinner was ready. As the kids came down the steps, Sean stopped and gave me a hug. "I love you, Aunt Maureen."

The sincerity and innocence in the hug of my six-year-old nephew simultaneously hurt and soothed my heart.

When my brother came home from work, Maryann told him what happened. I felt ashamed that I brought this terrible circus into their lives. My brother simply smiled, came over to give me a hug, and expressed his relief that I was with them. Christopher was not an intrusive man, but the concern in his eyes as he told me how sorry he was that I had to go through all of that reminded me how fortunate I was to be so loved.

When he quickly changed from his work clothes and stepped into his role as Emily's daddy and Maryann's husband, I sat back and watched what was clearly their nightly family ritual. I internally questioned if I was as good of a mom to Kayla as they were to Emily. Did Kayla have memories of family time or were we always running from softball game to softball game? I beat myself up for a few minutes, then decided I needed to sleep. But actually falling asleep was impossible.

CHAPTER 6

She Is . . . Slipping Away

**"Something's wrong, shut the light,
heavy thoughts tonight."
"Enter Sandman" by Metallica**

IN LESS THAN THREE DAYS, I HAD SYSTEMATI-cally checked off items from a bucket list I'd never written. I'd experienced the numbness of waking up emotionally deaf, the desperation of checking into a clinic, and the terror of possibly having to come to terms with the fact that I might never feel happy and whole. But those three things combined didn't compare to what awaited me. And it would be, by far, the very worst.

Falling into bed exhausted each night, I simply wanted to close my eyes and leave the day behind for just a few hours. My mind, it seemed, had other plans. It was as if laying my head on the pillow sent a signal to my brain that said, "Now it's time to introduce her to our friend, mental torture."

One . . . two . . . three . . . four . . . five . . . six . . .

EYES OPEN! Turn to the left side, please.

One . . . two . . . three . . . four . . . five . . .

EYES OPEN! Turn to the middle and try again.

One . . . two . . . three . . .

EYES OPEN! Let's go to the right side now.

There it was again, that thumping in my ears and chest. My heart was beating too hard and too fast.

Please God, don't let me have a heart attack. My blood pressure must be so high. Oh God, if I fall asleep, I'll have a stroke. How much can my body take before it gives up? I'm so tired and I just want to sleep.

TURN TO THE LEFT SIDE, PLEASE!

I'm so ashamed. Those people, their illnesses, their stories. I'm not one of them. I can't be one of them. What's happening to me? I'm losing this fight. Maybe I'm not supposed to win it.

MIDDLE!

What will this do to Kayla? I have no home, I've lost a business, I have no money, I'm irresponsible. I was a terrible wife, I'm a horrible mother, a failure as a daughter, and a burden.

SWITCH TO THE RIGHT NOW

He never said he was sorry. Why? How hard would it have been to just say, "I'm so sorry for everything I did? It was me. I was sick." *That little girl. I didn't take care of her. I pushed her away, and thought if I just forgot about her, everything would be all right. I'm so stupid . . .*

SWITCH LEFT!

Stop! Stop! Stop! I can't stop my mind from thinking! I'm so tired.

BACK TO THE MIDDLE!

You coward! What kind of person are you? How can you do this to your family?

GO TO THE RIGHT SIDE!

I know why this is happening. It's because I used to wish he would die. But I didn't know what else would make him stop. I was just scared. God is punishing me for wishing he would die.

SWITCH LEFT!

That artist guy from the group. I can't even remember his name. He's going to walk in with a gun tomorrow, I just know it.

SWITCH MIDDLE!

"Say something, I'm giving up on you. Sorry that I couldn't get to you. Anywhere I would follow you. Say something, I'm giving up on you . . ." I can't stop singing that song. I should hate CJ for everything he's done to me. So why do I feel guilty for leaving? Why do I feel like he isn't truly this terrible man?

SWITCH!

I still can't believe we never found the shoe that flew off my foot when I was hit by that car. That has to be forty years ago. Where could the shoe have gone?

SWITCH!

Help me. I'm so ashamed. What if I never find my way back?

SWITCH!

Okay, close your eyes. One . . . two . . . three . . . open! OPEN! OPEN! Why can't I stop them from opening?

SWITCH!

What did Tessa call me? A fragile warrior? I hate the way that sounds. It's like someone who perpetually treads water because she's too afraid to swim.

SWITCH!

I was supposed to be the one who succeeded. All the sacrifices my mother made for me so I could be more, have more, and achieve more; she wasted all that time and effort on me. Why did she have me? She gave up her life, her dreams, and her goals and I've failed her.

SWITCH!

I'm sorry, Kayla. I've let you down, especially the past four years. I thought if I left an unhappy marriage and showed you what a really happy relationship looked like and how important it was to follow your happiness, I was being a good mother. Instead, I blew your world apart, didn't I? Emotionally, I abandoned you, didn't I? I failed you . . .

SWITCH!

*One . . . two . . . three . . . four . . . five . . . six . . . seven . . .
I'm counting higher . . . If I just keep my eyes closed I'll fall asleep .
. . eight . . . nine . . . just keep your eyes closed, Maureen . . . don't
peek at the clock . . . ten . . . eleven . . . OPEN!*

SWITCH!

*I will never be able to go on Facebook again. Seeing my friends
and their happy, successful lives is just too painful. I'm always the
happy, funny, encouraging friend. I post the funny e-cards and send
my support when I see my friends, or family members are struggling.*

Now what would I say?

*"I know you think I've been this incredible funny, supportive,
insightful person, but guess what? I'm a phony liar who is having a nervous breakdown! LMAO! Can you believe it? You've been
friends with a depressed, anxiety-ridden lunatic who is destroying
her family and you never knew it! TTYL XOXOXO!"*

SWITCH!

*Kayla, I'm sorry. If you only knew how much I wish I had been
the mother I thought I could be. You deserved so much better.*

SWITCH!

I have to pee. I can't. I'll wake up the whole house. Shit!

SWITCH!

Please stop! God, please turn off my thoughts off!

SWITCH!

*Thump . . . thump . . . thump . . . thump . . . thump . . .
thump. I know I'll never see the morning. I'm going to die in my*

sleep. Maybe that's best. Maybe in just one quick second, the lights will go out. Maybe that's the only way to stop this. Is that suicide ideation? Jesus! I am one of them!

SWITCH!

I'm going to get fired. They think I'm irresponsible. They think I'm completely unqualified to do my job. I'm not even capable of being an assistant anymore. There isn't one thing in my life right now I can claim as a success. I've wasted my life, haven't I?

SWITCH!

If I don't stop crying, I'll look like a frog in therapy tomorrow. I'm so ugly when I cry. Who am I kidding? I'm just ugly.

SWITCH!

Kayla. God, please help her. I'm failing and she needs you. Please, don't let her be like me. Please help her recognize her intelligence, beauty, and the countless other ways she is such an incredible young woman. Please don't let my weakness weigh her down.

SWITCH!

Technically, I'm homeless. I couldn't afford to live on my own even if I wanted to. How embarrassing for my daughter, for my family. At every turn, I'm a failure. How did this happen? How did I fall so far when I was so sure I was finally living a successful life?

It's because I'm stupid.

My head is so far up my ass, I believe the bullshit I tell myself. I believed that a pitiful person such as myself could leave the past behind and keep moving forward to a better life. Instead, I have fallen lower than ever before. I should have just taken the city job my mother always told me to take. She said they offered security, benefits, and a pension. Nope, I wanted to work on Wall Street. I wanted to be the exact opposite of all the women in my family. And I am. They own their own homes and live independently. I now live with my brother and his family. I should have just driven into a tree.

SWITCH!

"I got sunshine on a cloudy day. When it's cold outside, I got the month of May . . . my girl." I love you infinity times, which means my love goes on and on for you, forever and ever. I'm sorry.

SWITCH!

When did I stop being enough, CJ? I trusted you with everything. Every embarrassing story, every shame, every secret. I believed you were my best friend. I believed you when you said you would never hurt me, always love me and always be there for me. I felt safe with you. Why? If you fell out of love with me, why couldn't you just be honest? Why did you turn so cruel? Why didn't I leave sooner?

SWITCH!

One . . . two . . . three . . . four . . . doesn't matter.

Eyes open, eyes closed.

God, help my family understand I didn't mean for this to happen. I'm sorry I've failed them. I'm sorry I'm weak. Please make them believe I've tried. I'm just so tired, but I can't shut down. My mind simply won't allow it. The thumping in my chest, the pound-

ing in my ears, the random thoughts that seem to be running on an endless loop through my mind all make sleep impossible.

Was this how it felt to descend into madness?

CHAPTER 7

She Is . . . Unworthy

"Won't let nobody hurt you, I'll stand by you."
"I'll Stand By You" by The Pretenders

"YOU KEPT YOUR PROMISE. IT'S A NEW WEEK and you made it back and you're early again. I continue to be impressed!" Tessa caught me sitting in the group room alone, staring at the carpet, and I jumped at the sound of her voice.

I wanted to respond, "Don't be." I couldn't stand being in my own skin and the off switch for my mind was broken.

"How was your weekend? Did you get any sleep?" she asked.

I wanted to tell her that my heart was beating so hard, I was afraid I was going to have a heart attack or stroke. I wanted to tell her I tried at least a hundred times to close my eyes and count, hoping that at the very least, boredom would make me fall asleep, but my brain wouldn't shut down. I wanted to tell her it felt as if my body was shaking internally and I sat up at times rocking back and forth, crying and praying for morning to come. I wanted to tell her it was the longest night of my entire life. But I didn't.

"I dozed off here and there, but nothing consistent. Maybe an hour and a half each night."

"That's not good, Maureen. Our priority is to get you sleeping and eating again. It may take a while, but as you go through the program, you'll learn some skills to help you relax and quiet your mind. The first week is the roughest. Just hang in there, okay?" I nodded and Tessa quickly said she'd see me later as she took off down the hallway.

I was relieved to be alone. Oddly enough, that was the first moment my heart didn't feel as if it was in a boxing match. Listening to the rhythm of the clinic calmed me and distracted the ping pong ball of thoughts bouncing around my mind. I wanted to sob. I wanted to unlock everything in my body, mind, and heart and let it just fill the room. I wanted to wail; I wanted to cry a guttural cry; I wanted someone to experience my pain, if only to see the power it had over me. Perhaps if someone else saw it, touched it, understood it, they could convince me there was a way to release it without it killing me and everyone I knew and loved.

I closed my eyes and became absorbed in the quiet of the room. *Why couldn't I find this sense of stillness last night?*

Slowly, the room began to fill with my fellow group members and our clinician came in to begin our first session of the day. The clinician running the session was Kelly. She seemed to be in her early 40s and after five minutes, I understood that she was absolutely the "take no shit" clinician. I was both terrified and intrigued.

Again, I was not called upon to process or share anything, and I was grateful. Those who did process expressed feelings that ranged from calm and content to rage and impatience with what was going on in their lives . . . or in their heads. I simply had no capacity to show any interest or empathy. Internally, I still felt barren and my usual well of endless compassion was experiencing a drought.

Our ninety-minute session ended, we took a break for lunch, then headed to our education group. Education was much bigger than the morning group. I found a chair in a corner and settled in comfortably and unassumingly until Kelly walked in. She was also running this group today and as she surveyed the room, she asked out loud, "Can we please spread out a bit? I don't want anyone sitting in the corner." I looked up and stopped breathing.

"Maureen, I can't see you back there. Would you please scoot your chair up?"

I smiled, nodded, and dragged my chair up closer. Kelly smiled back at me with a satisfied look on her face and began talking about the importance of support systems.

"So, did everyone do the homework I assigned?"

Homework? We got homework? I was getting that awful stomach pain, like the one you got on the first day of school when you realized none of your friends were in your homeroom class. Through my growing anxiety attack, I realized the majority of the group had not done their homework assignment . . . and Kelly was *not* impressed.

"Hmmm. Okay, well, if no one was able to do the assignment at home, I guess we're going to have to do it right now." A low grumble spread across the room, but Kelly didn't skip a beat. "I want each of you to think about the people in your life that are part of your support system, choose one of them, and tell the group about the person you've chosen."

God, I hoped that didn't include me. I wasn't here for the assignment. I didn't know about it, so she couldn't possibly think I should . . .

"Maureen, I'd like to begin with you. I know you're new to the group and it's only your second day. I believe this would be an easy way for you to begin to get comfortable sharing something about yourself that isn't too intrusive, and doesn't require anything more than the name of a person and whatever you're comfortable telling us about them. Are you okay with that?"

I reminded myself that I'd promised Tessa I would do whatever was asked of me.

I nodded and took a deep breath. The entire group's eyes were on me and I looked up at Kelly. She nodded her head and slightly smiled.

"If I had to pick someone, it would be Aunt Kathy. She is my mom's younger sister, but we are only nine years apart. She has always been more of an older sister to me than an aunt."

Kelly was very slowly nodding her head. She spoke clearly and deliberately, choosing every word carefully. "Can you elaborate on why you picked your aunt? Has she done something apart from other people within your support system that separates her? Anything you feel comfortable sharing?"

My gaze shifted from Kelly down to the rug and my leg started to shake. What had she done? What was it about her? What did I say? How did I say it? I could feel tears forming because I knew what I was about to say was something I'd never said out loud.

"She saved my life."

As I looked back up at Kelly, two tears fell. I bit my lip and looked away . . .

I was five years old and my aunt was fourteen. My mother was dating Bob, the man who would adopt me and become my dad. They were on a double date with my mom's cousin, Ellen, and Ellen's husband, James. I called her Aunt Ellen even though technically she was my cousin, because she was my godmother. Aunt Kathy and I were staying at Aunt Ellen's house. My recollection of that night's events was from the viewpoint of that five-year-old:

I'm asleep in a big bed.

I hear a man's voice and I start to wake up. "If you wake her up, I'll kill her."

I don't know that voice. I freeze. Suddenly every sound in the quiet house is amplified.

I am afraid to breathe too loud.

Is my aunt crying?

I'm lying on my right side and I open one eye. The lamp is on.

My aunt is on her left side, facing me. She is crying.

"Shhhhhh . . . go back to sleep," she whispers. She's crying.

I close my eyes.

It's quiet.

I open both my eyes. I'm alone.

Did I fall asleep?

Where's Aunt Kathy?

I'm scared.

I slip off the bed and crawl on my hands and knees out of the bedroom.

Please don't let the floor creak. The wood floor is so cold. This hall is so dark.

My knees hurt.

I peek around the kitchen doorway.

My aunt is locking the back door, then walks to an open drawer.

There is a knife in her hand.

She moves her hand into the drawer then closes the drawer.

Where is that man? Is he still here?

I want Mommy.

I'm still on my belly. I slide backward to the bedroom. Be quiet.

I wish I was bigger. I have to get in the bed faster. It's so high.

I slowly put myself back under the covers.

I'm still afraid to breathe too loud.

I hear my aunt walk into the room.

She gets me out of bed and gives me my box of Mr. Potato Head pieces. We're now standing in the hallway. Aunt Kathy is talking on the phone.

The box falls and the pieces smash on the wooden floor.

The crash is so loud. The pieces go everywhere.

I jump. My aunt screams out loud. "STOP, MISSY! PLEASE STOP!"

My aunt is crying as she's talking on the phone.

Then I'm sitting on a wooden chair, looking up at a desk with a smiling police officer.

"If it wasn't for my aunt, I wouldn't be here."

As I sat there I thought back to when I finally asked my aunt about that night. I thought it might have been a dream or a false memory. She couldn't believe I remembered so much. She told me the adults forgot to lock the back door that night and an intruder came in after I went to bed. He grabbed a knife from the kitchen drawer, brought her into the bedroom, and assaulted her. He threatened to kill me, so she didn't make a sound as he brutalized her. It wasn't a dream; it was all true.

"She is the bravest person I've ever known." I was ashamed as I said those words. Another woman in my family who sacrificed herself for a little girl who grew up to be a weak woman.

I wasn't worthy of such sacrifices.

CHAPTER 8

She Is . . . Sidestepping

"I miss that town, I miss their faces."
"Photograph" by Nickelback

"I HEARD YOU CONTRIBUTED TODAY IN THE education session." I was beginning to think Tessa had radar as I turned around and saw her head poking out from her office. But it made me smile, which was a rarity right now.

"Well, I promised you I would do anything that was asked of me. Kelly asked me to participate, and I kept my promise. Did I want to? No. But I promised, and right now the only thing I have control over is keeping my word, so I've decided that's where I will start."

Tessa looked right at me confirming my decision and said

"There she is . . . the warrior! Do you have time to chat for a bit?"

I sat in Tessa's office and glanced around at the photos of

her family, the organized chaos on her desk, and the inspirational sayings on her wall. We were sitting face to face and although she was smiling, she seemed to be struggling with what she wanted to say.

"I was reading over your intake file. Pretty intense stuff," Tessa said nervously.

I shrugged. "It's been interesting." I felt like we were preparing to waltz and I'd just responded to Tessa's bow with a curtsy.

"How did you think you were able to manage that? How did you manage to deal with so much from such a young age? You're a walking trauma, Maureen. I don't say that as an insult. Quite the contrary. The fact that you are here at all defines your strength."

"A therapist once told me that your sense of safety, of being loved, develops in the first five years of your life," I explained. "The first five years of my life were great, to my recollection. I was surrounded by family members who loved me and took care of me, so if what she said is true, then that certainly helped."

I didn't want to talk about what I'd dealt with at a young age. I was not here to discuss my past. I was here because of CJ.

"As things changed, I didn't know anything else, so I adjusted and existed in the world I was in. I think most kids do that, don't you?"

I was hoping to get Tessa to agree so that we could leave this part of our conversation behind. I knew where she was trying to steer this and I wouldn't allow it.

"Whether their life is good or bad, a kid doesn't have a choice. I lived on a block with a lot of kids, so I had friends. School was fun because I met more friends and had great teachers. There were a lot of distractions. And whether I had a good day, bad day, or went to bed feeling sick or sad, I told myself I was luckier than a lot of other kids who didn't have friends, or a home, or food to eat. And when that didn't work, I would think about what kind of life I would have once I was grown up and didn't have to live with . . . him."

Tessa's hands were clasped together with her chin resting on both index fingers, her body rocking ever so slowly. "You were quite a remarkable young girl, Maureen. You were using skills as a child that most adults have a hard time grasping. It's what has gotten you this far in life."

"All I can say is that I tried to have as much fun as I could whenever possible. What kid doesn't?" *Just agree with me, Tessa, so we can move on.*

Tessa nodded her head in agreement, and my memory of being a young girl playing with her childhood friends made me smile.

"And I would hardly call myself a remarkable young girl or a warrior. I wasn't unique. I was just trying to be a normal kid."

I grew up in Bensonhurst, Brooklyn. I know everyone feels

like the place where they grew up was the best place in the world, with the best people, and the best food—but in my case, it was true. Bensonhurst in the '60s and '70s was a one-of-a-kind neighborhood. Punchball, Stickball, Skellies, Stoop Ball, Spin the Bottle, Cocolevio, Mr. Softee, the King Kong Ride, Whip Ride, and summertime block parties were just a few of the stored memories of everything good in my childhood.

Just about every family we were friends with had a last name that ended in a vowel, and the smell of Sunday sauce traveled from one end of the block to the other. One of the families on our block had ten kids. And there was Ruthie, a scary old woman who lived in a big, rundown house right in the middle of our block. At the age of ten, I was hit by a car and lost one of my shoes in her bushes. It was never found.

We played and ran around each day until the streetlights came on or our parents "called" for us—usually standing on a porch or leaning out of a window screaming our name or giving a distinct whistle. We played RCK (Run, Catch, Kiss) in the big grassy lot that was next to the nursing home.

Every Friday night, there was a gathering at one of our houses to watch the Friday night TV lineup: *Let's Make A Deal, That Girl, The Brady Bunch, The Partridge Family, The Odd Couple.* And after your friends left, if you were lucky, Love American Style and Don Kirschner's Rock Concert.

Our fathers were electricians, cops, construction workers,

and businessmen, with a few wise guys sprinkled in the mix, and most of our moms were stay-at-home mothers. Those who had a front lawn mowed it faithfully every weekend, and those who didn't hosed down the concrete in front of their home. We sat on the stoop of one of my friends' houses and ate fresh figs from the tree in her front yard, and on hot summer days, we ran through the water from the open hydrant or under hoses hung by one of our mothers from a porch.

I loved living on that block. I loved all of those kids and I still do, even to this day. Without even knowing it, they all contributed to saving my life. I loved being a part of something that was bigger and happier than what was going on in my home. It made me believe that when I grew up, I could have more and live a happy life. But until that time came, I was just happy being Missy from 84th Street.

"Children are incredibly resilient, aren't they? They can find ways to latch onto the good and use it to get them through the bad." Tessa's voice snapped me back to our conversation.

"They are," I agreed, "but I think children are stubborn, sprinkled with determination overall. They want their way, and they spend their time trying to figure out how to get it."

Tessa pushed back. "Stubborn? Really? Why stubborn instead of resilient?"

"Because in spite of everything, the thought that always ran through my head when things started happening and I truly wanted to give up was that I couldn't let him win. Stubborn. There was also the hope that the man who married my mother would come back. If I gave up, there would never be a chance of seeing my dad again. Determination."

"Well, now that you're here, we can start to deal with what happened with your dad. It will take some . . ." I cut Tessa off.

"No. I don't have to deal with any of that. I put myself in therapy years ago to deal with my relationship with my father. Bringing that up will accomplish nothing. I just want to deal with what's happening right now. That is the past. Done and over. There is no point in revisiting it."

Although most of my little chat with Tessa brought some welcome relief and even a few smiles, the mere thought of revisiting my relationship with my father made me feel like I wanted to jump out of my own skin. He had nothing to do with what was happening to me right now. This chaos . . . this breakdown . . . it was my fault. No one else was responsible for it. If Tessa thought she was giving me an out by trying to pin this on my past and that I would allow it, she was wrong. I'd done this to myself. I was to blame.

"Uhhhh . . . okay, then. Somehow I doubt that is the case, but if you're unwilling or not ready or feel no need to go there, then we'll just concentrate on getting you back to level."

I was quietly relieved that Tessa gave me an out.

"Level? What do you mean by level?" I was fading fast. The

lack of sleep and lack of appetite were starting to catch up to me.

"Sleeping regularly, eating regularly, and getting your anxiety under control."

As I picked up my coat to leave, the only thought running through my mind was a short and sweet, "Good luck with that."

CHAPTER 9

She Is . . . Ashamed

"And you know wherever I am I'll come running . . ."
"You Got A Friend" by Carole King

ONE SLEEPLESS NIGHT AFTER ANOTHER. DAYS turned into nights, and nights back into days. I'd been a part of the program for three weeks. Every morning was the same routine. Alarm went off, I made my bed, took a shower, drank a cup of tea, sat on the couch, stared into the backyard, cried, then left for the clinic. It took two weeks to get me serious-ly onboard and working toward "level," and that was only be-cause Tessa warned me that if I didn't start engaging more, there was a real possibility of them having to hospitalize me. I'd lost too much weight too quickly and the guilt I carried about my daughter returning from school for Christmas break to a moth-er who was, quite literally, a basket case was unbearable in every sense of the word.

Her father and I agreed to tell her together. I was waiting for her at her dad's house the day she came home for Christmas break. As she sat across the table from me sharing her college stories and the relief of having her finals behind her, my heart was slowly breaking from the weight of the guilt of what we were about to tell her.

She doesn't deserve what we're about to say. She should be allowed to simply exist in her twenty-year-old world. The only things she should be burdened with are what to wear to her next party, cleaning her apartment and getting through finals. I'm sorry, Kayla. I'm sorry for what is about to be said.

Mike took the lead. "So, Mom and I wanted to talk to you about something that's going on."

The smile, excitement and relief just to be home that was on her face dissolved, and in its place a blank, frozen expression. Kayla looked away from her dad, and locked eyes with me. *Look! Look at what you've done.*

As I began to tell her as gently as I could that I had to take a leave of absence because I wasn't well, her eyes stayed locked on mine. I didn't go into detail about what had happened with CJ, but in my heart I knew she could read between the lines. I tried to reassure her all would work out, but the life I watched slowly disappear from her eyes was what made my tears begin to quietly fall. *How dare you cry! You are literally shattering her entire world, dragging her into your shitshow of a life. Pull yourself together and be the mother she needs you to be . . . the mother you have never been.*

Outwardly, she handled the news very well. But I knew I'd strapped an anvil to my daughter's back. She now had a front row seat not only to the consequences of a part of her family's legacy, but to my emotional vulnerability. The tightrope I walked between the fragility of my emotional state and the shame of having my daughter step up to the plate and watch over me caused my mind to wander and ask the question most would find unthinkable: would she truly be better off without me?

This was a time in her life when I should be guiding her, supporting her, advising her, and celebrating her accomplishments. Instead, she'd become my caretaker. Driving me to doctor's appointments, sitting with me and watching TV at night to keep me company, and waiting for my call as soon as I left the clinic to reassure her I was okay.

Christmas was always my favorite holiday. Once we had Kayla, Christmas went into overdrive. Mike decorated every inch of the outside and I decorated the inside, and our neighbors dubbed us the gingerbread house. I remember her first Christmas; she was eight months old. Mike had just finished putting up the lights around all of the windows and was decorating the bushes. I brought Kayla up on the bed to look at the lights, and Mike was standing on the other side of the window. Kayla pressed her little chubby hands against the pane and started banging on the glass, squealing and laughing as she watched her dad decorate the bush in front of her. I wanted every Christmas to be that magical for Kayla.

This Christmas left me in such a state of depression and anxiety, I spent most of the Eve on the top floor of my mother's house sitting on the couch, crying while my family celebrated below. My daughter sat next to me, held my hand, told me I would be okay, handed me tissues, hugged me tight, and continued to whisper how much she loved me. I didn't deserve her, and I am sickened at the thought that this was a memory that would stick with her forever.

Once the holidays were behind us, I was relieved when my daughter called me one night to tell me she was going out with friends. That was what I wanted for her; to be twenty years old, home from college, and enjoying the friends she grew up with. That was all I'd ever wanted.

I decided I was going to make a cup of tea, curl up with my binder of handouts given to us at the clinic every day, and find some new "skills" to help me cope with the endless stream of thoughts that polluted my mind. As I opened the nightstand drawer to look for my glasses, I realized there were pictures scattered across the bottom of the drawer. I picked one up to take a look. When I turned it over, I was startled by the faces looking back at me.

I was staring at two young girls in the apartment where I grew up. Their arms were slung over each other's shoulders and they were bent over, laughing. It was me and my best friend, Ann. It was the contrast in our height that made us dissolve into giggles because one tried stretching up and the other was slouching down. We were the very best of friends. We were each other's lifelines. Most importantly, she was the second person to save my life.

My father loved Ann. She called him Pop, sat on his lap, and laughed at his jokes—all the things I refused to do. According to him, if I'd treated him as well as Ann, I probably would have avoided getting punished as much as I did. In his mind, she was respectful and playful. She was his Annie Fannie.

The thing that brought me the most pleasure was that she wasn't any of those things when it came to my father. Her sole purpose was always to get me out of the house and away from him. Looking back, it astounded me that someone so young would put herself on the line the way she did for me.

"I can't go out." Most of my friends gave up on ever trying to make plans with me. My father would usually wait until they showed up at the door, then find some ridiculous reason to punish me. Eventually, even if they asked if I wanted to go roller skating or to a movie, it was usually followed with, "We know you won't be able to, but we figured we'd at least ask if you wanted to come with us."

Ann never gave up.

"What did you do now? Forget to wear your slippers? Polish your toenails red?" Ann was the only friend who understood the dynamic of my relationship with my dad and the asinine excuses he could come up with just to keep me in the house.

"I didn't dry the dishes. He told me to dry them and I didn't dry them that second. He said since I didn't have time to do as I was told, I obviously had no time to be with my friends."

"Is your mom home?" I knew why Ann was asking that question.

"No. She just left for bingo." I hated bingo nights.

"Okay. Start getting dressed and I'll be there in fifteen minutes. Fuck him and his dishes. You're going out."

I hung up with Ann and did what she said. I started putting my pants on when the banging on my bedroom door made me stumble and fall.

"WHY DO YOU HAVE THIS DOOR BLOCKED?"

I wasn't allowed to have a door lock on my bedroom door, but I'd devised a homemade warning system by keeping my closet door open all the time. When open, the closet door rested in front of my bedroom door so when my father tried to come in without knocking, the doors would bang together and I'd have at least a second or two to cover up.

"I SWEAR TO GOD, MAUREEN, I'M GOING TO RIP THIS DAMN DOOR OFF THE HINGES!"

"I'm sorry. I was putting clothes away in the closet." I closed the closet door and he came bursting into my room.

"Did you tell Ann you weren't going out tonight?" My dad was 6'4", about 250 pounds, and almost completely bald. He was an electrician for an alarm company that installed bank alarms. Most people found him very witty and a great storyteller. No one knew him as the menacing bully I lived with every day. No one knew the truly horrible man he was.

"Yes, I told her. She's coming over to hang for a little while."

"Good. I love my Annie Fannie. She's my sweetheart." I hated the way he called her Annie Fannie. It made my skin crawl. "If you were more like her, things could be much nicer for you around here. You could get a lot more of what you want, but you insist on disobeying me. You could learn a thing or two about respect and how a daughter should treat her father from Annie Fannie."

I could learn a thing or two, I thought. *And you could learn a thing or two about being a decent human being, you baldheaded, fat ass, Uncle Fester-looking fuckface.*

After giving me the once-over, he walked out and I was alone again. I was just getting my socks on when I heard the hallway door slam shut and Ann bounding up the steps, crashing through our front door. I cracked open my bedroom door.

"Hey, Pop! Where's she at?" Ann always called my father Pop because she knew how much he loved it.

"Hey, sweetheart. Come give your Pop a hug and a kiss hello."

Ann was more than just my best friend. She knew what would happen when my mom went to bingo, just like I knew what happened when she said her dad was on a rampage. The nights I'd go to her house, hang with her and her sisters, and eat dinner with them, he was always calm and polite, and I felt like I was the gatekeeper for them. Tonight was her turn to be the gatekeeper, and I watched her sit on my father's lap and give him a big hug and kiss. I knew she hated him.

"You and me have to have a little conversation." She smiled at him. "You can't punish her tonight because I just finished my punishment. You know my dad won't let me hang out unless Maureen is with me. She's the only friend he trusts. C'mon, Pop! Do it for me. Do it for your Annie Fannie, puhleeeeeze?" She hugged him harder and gave him a huge kiss on the head. He was putty in her hands.

"Maureen! Come out here!" I waited a second or two, then calmly strolled out of my bedroom.

I looked at my father, then over at Ann, and I could see the smirk start to form on her lips before she quickly turned back to my father.

"Well, Pop? You gonna tell her or am I?" She tilted her chin down with a playful pout on her face and placed her forehead against his forehead.

"You know I can't say no to my little Annie Fannie." He was eating up the attention, holding her tightly around her waist as she sat firmly on his lap with her arms draped around his neck.

"You can go out for two hours. Be back in this house by 9:00. Don't make me sit out on that porch waiting for you."

"I won't. Thank you."

I glanced over at Ann, who was now looking me straight in the eye. She raised an eyebrow, smiled triumphantly, and in less than three minutes, we were outside, riding our bikes to hang out with our friends.

"How do you do that? How do you sit on his lap and let him hug you like that?"

"How do you sit and listen to my mother go on and on about how horrible my dad is, or hang out with me and my sisters so my dad won't beat the crap out of us?"

"I do it because you're my best friend and I love you." I loved her like a sister.

"And that's how I do it. I love you, too. Fuck 'em both, Maureen. For two hours, we don't have to deal with either of them. Let's go hang out and have fun."

Thirty-five years later, I was lying in bed, my mind jumping from memory to memory. I looked back at the picture of those two girls and smiled through the tears that began to roll down my cheeks. I loved the memories I had of my sweet, funny, ball-sy friend, and I missed her. I wished she was here. She would know how to quiet down all the ruminating thoughts that occupied my mind and kept me awake all night so I couldn't sleep.

She would understand why I had to enter this program. She would look me squarely in the eye, raise her eyebrow, smile her crooked smile, and wink her approval. She'd sit next to me, hug me, tell me everything would be okay, and convince me to say all the things I've held in too long. We'd sing the songs we loved when we hung out on my porch on the days she could break away from her own hell, just to try to get me to laugh.

I laid awake, trying to find the girl I was when my sweet friend needed protection. I tried to recall how I was just as brash and fearless while in the company of her father. We were only thirteen, brave, and bound together by the reality that the men who were supposed to protect us were the men that seemed hell-bent on destroying us. And we were just as hell-bent on making sure they didn't.

I closed my eyes, envisioned her smile, and heard her crazy laugh. I chuckled inwardly at the memory of how she'd called everyone she loved babe, and everyone she didn't a twat. I started to drift off, quietly singing an old song from a Paul Stanley album. KISS was her favorite band and we wore out that album.

For the first time in what seemed like forever, I slept through the night.

CHAPTER 10

She Is . . . Revealed

"When the walls come tumblin' tumblin' down."
"Crumbling Down" by John Mellencamp

"OKAY, WHO WOULD LIKE TO BEGIN PROCESS this morning?" Kelly was our group leader that morning, and she was carefully surveying the room. There were some mornings when three or four group members came in chomping at the bit to process with the group, and other mornings when no one wanted to look up from the floor.

In the weeks I'd been here, I'd chosen to fly under the radar but not appear uninterested in processing. Because I made it a point to arrive at least a half hour before group began, I was always the first person in our room. As my fellow group members entered, conversations began and people started sharing before our session actually started. I listened and quickly outlined in my mind who I felt needed to process the most.

When we reached the moment our clinician asked who would like to begin, I would patiently wait to see if a group member volunteered. If not, I would encouragingly say something to the effect of, "Ted/Marilyn/Sean, why don't you process what you were talking about/what happened last night?" Basically, I threw someone else under the bus so that I wasn't called upon.

After check-in, Kelly looked around. "So does anyone have something they would like to process?" Crickets. No one was making eye contact. No one wanted to begin.

"Nobody needs to process today? No one has anything they need to discuss, or share, or get off their chest?" Kelly was sitting back in her chair, surveying the group, hands in her lap, and fingers interlocked. Just as I was about to choose our speaker, Kelly changed the game.

"Well, then, I guess it's my pick."

Uh-oh. No gentle throwing anyone else under the bus today. I stared at the rug, my leg shaking uncontrollably. This must be what Russian Roulette feels like. The room was silent, but I knew what was coming.

"How about it, Maureen? Ready to do this?" All eyes looked up and were on me. I, again, remembered that promise I'd made the first day I walked into this clinic. I was annoyed and found it ironic that the guilt and shame that were part of my breakdown were the same things that would make me keep my promise.

"Sure." I shrugged and half smiled. Part of me felt like it was time.

"All right. Tell us what's going on. When I took pulse this morning, the two emotions you said you were experiencing were guilt and shame. Can you elaborate? Why the shame?" Kelly had a way of phrasing her questions so that they came across as requests that couldn't be refused.

I took a deep breath. Everyone looked at me. I hesitated, but then just let my thoughts escape my mouth. "Because I have let my family down. I'm ashamed that I wasn't strong enough and allowed myself to get sick in this way. I'm ashamed that my daughter has a mother who is weak and isn't there for her. I'm ashamed that my mother has a daughter who is a burden and can't get her life together. I'm ashamed that I'm the oldest and now it's my brothers who have to help me. I'm ashamed of things I've done, people I've hurt, decisions I've made. There's not a whole lot I'm not ashamed of."

I was speaking a lot more comfortably than I thought I would. I didn't mind speaking in front of people, but I didn't think I still had the ability to do it. Everything that was Maureen seemed to disappear. Apparently, my gift of gab had not.

"Can you explain to the group how you let yourself get sick?" Kelly air quoted 'let yourself get sick.'

"I've just never been as strong as the other women in my family. I've never been able to just keep moving forward. I mean, my situation is not unique, especially in my family. But they got up every morning, went to work, came home, made dinner, took care of their families, and never complained. They managed to keep their lives and their families together without any outside help. I wasn't built with that type of fortitude."

"So what I'm hearing is that because you chose to get help, you are weak. Is that correct?"

"Just speaking for myself, in comparison to my family members, yes. I let everything fall apart. None of them have ever fallen apart; they've fallen down, but they've always picked themselves up and moved forward. Me? I had to leave work, remove myself from my home and relationship, and face the fact that I am incapable of getting out of my own way."

No one was saying anything. Their eyes were fixated on me, probably because that was the most I'd shared about myself since the day I'd walked in. Kelly was slowly nodding her head up and down.

"You said they kept their families together. Are you divorced?" I was sitting next to Sean and he leaned over the way friends do when they were having a serious chat.

"My husband and I have been separated and living apart for five or six years now. We haven't made it official, but for all intents and purposes, we are no longer married. I moved out and am . . . was . . . living with my boyfriend."

"Okay, so you're the only woman in your family who has

ended her marriage . . ." Sean was nodding and commenting in a way that suggested he'd figured out part of the problem and understood some of what I was struggling with. He didn't.

"No, I'm not the only one." Sean furrowed his brow and the expression on his face quickly registered confusion. "The majority of the women in my family are either divorced, separated, or single."

Before I could continue, Kelly interjected. "Maureen, when you say they were able to keep their families together, are you referring to staying married or is there something else you can share to help the group understand what you are talking about?"

I was looking at her, but I could see my heart beating through my shirt.

"What I mean is they were able to function and move past the things that happened in their lives. I don't know how else to explain it." That was a lie. I knew exactly how to explain it. I knew what I was saying made absolutely no sense to the group because I was talking in circles. But the words that needed to be said didn't seem to be able to roll off my tongue.

"What things did they move past?" Marilyn chimed in.

I could feel myself internally go from four to ten on the anxiety scale and I was suddenly thinking, "It's none of your Goddamn business!" I was very aware of the anger that was quickly swelling internally. I was biting my lip the way a mother did when she was trying to control her anger toward her children. I looked to Kelly for support. We made direct eye contact; she would nudge, but never pushed. I realized it was time to get to work. There were no more lifelines, no more passes. It was time to dive in.

Deep breath . . . three . . . two . . . one . . .

"Sexual abuse. Every woman in my family has been sexually abused, assaulted, or both. I was sexually abused for many years by my father. It started when I was six and continued until I was fifteen." I was also sexually assaulted by the grocer who had a store up the block from my house on 84th street, my family doctor, and by an ex-boyfriend, but I didn't want to keep one-upping myself.

Sean sighed heavily, then sat up to speak. "Maureen, why do you feel you are weaker than all of them? Is it because you're here?" I really liked Sean. He was able to be both logical and soothing at the same time, and he genuinely seemed to be a good, decent man. It was easy for me to forget that he'd tried to kill himself.

"Not just that . . ." I kept twirling my tissues around my fingers and my nose started running.

"Can you explain what it is then, Maureen?" As I looked up at Kelly, then Marilyn, and back down to the carpet, the tears started to fall steadily and the pain of everything I didn't want to say was pressing against my chest.

"I'm the one who told. I couldn't keep it in any longer. I told and my family exploded into a million pieces."

"No! Maureen, your family exploded into a million pieces because of what that pervert did to you, not because you told. If he hadn't been a pedophile, there wouldn't have been anything to tell." I heard what Marilyn was saying, but there was so much more to it.

Ted chimed in for the first time. "Maureen, you were six years old. You held it in for nine years. Opening your mouth probably saved your life. Look at how hard it's been for you, living and working through the truth. You got guts, Maureen. You should be proud you didn't keep it in. He's the one who should carry the shame and the guilt of abusing a little girl. You didn't do anything wrong."

Ted doesn't say much, and now after listening to his kind words, I felt silly when I remembered how I'd thought he was the one who was going to go postal the first day I met him. I appreciated their perspectives and their attempts to reassure me that I had no control over what occurred. But opening Pandora's Box all those years ago had done nothing but cause me and my family pain.

My mother sacrificed her happiness to have me. She fell in love with my biological father, and at the age of eighteen got pregnant. His family sent him away after the pregnancy was revealed, and when he returned, he met and became engaged to the woman who would be his wife. He was never a part of my life. Neither I, nor anyone in my family ever referred to him as my dad.

My mother was destined for bigger and better things. She was beautiful, outgoing, hardworking and well-liked by everyone who met her. She supported her mother, brother, and younger sister and was determined to find a way to get them out of the poverty they lived in most of their lives. She had a great job in New York that she acquired right out of high school. Getting pregnant wasn't part of the plan and it changed everything.

Back in the '60s, if you became pregnant without being married, it was shameful. You were labeled "that" kind of girl. Easy. A slut. My mom told me a story about how, almost a year after having me and giving up on the thought of ever dating, she finally said yes to going on a date after being repeatedly asked by a young man she knew. Once they were in his car, he expected to get lucky, and when she declined, he asked, "Why not? It's not like you haven't already done it." She was devastated. She thought this boy was someone nice who really liked her. Instead, he just wanted to get laid. She didn't date again. She simply worked hard, continued to support her family, and raised me.

I became her shadow. We did everything together. My recollections of being a young child who lived with my mom, grandmother, uncle, and aunt were always happy. My memory of the little house we rented was safe, fun, and a sweet part of my childhood.

When my mother met Bob, it was exciting for me and for my family as well. They were introduced by her cousin, Ellen. Ellen's husband, James, was Bob's friend and co-worker. My mother was the happiest I'd ever remembered seeing her. I loved sitting on the lid of the toilet, watching her put on her make-up, and then waiting to see what sparkly outfit she would wear when he came to pick her up for the company dances or out to dinner. And together, the three of us would go to Coney Island and the movies.

Bob was tall and handsome with a deep voice, and having my beautiful mom by his side completed a puzzle I never realized was missing an important piece. They held hands and adored one another. My favorite times were when we were in his car and someone would cut him off or do something ridiculous. He'd roll down his window and yell out, "You clown!" That was my queue to squeeze my head out of his window and yell, "Yeah, you clown!" He pretended the light in his car was magic and he'd command, "Magic light, turn on!" and the light would go on. Then he'd tell me, "Okay, you try it," and I would squeal when the light would come on at my bidding.

The day they got married, I felt like a princess because my mother looked like a queen marrying her king. I now had a daddy, another grandma and uncle, and a grandpa.

After returning from their honeymoon, Bob legally adopted me. Although I have absolutely no recollection of that day, I recalled my mother telling me when the judge called me up to sit in the seat next to him and asked me who my dad was, I smiled and pointed directly at Bob.

I was the luckiest girl in the entire world . . . for a short time, at least.

When we broke for lunch, I began to accept what I fought so hard to avoid; what I knew all along. My nervous breakdown wasn't just about CJ. He was merely a once shiny bow that wrapped the neat, little boxes I placed all the shameful moments of my life in which were about to be untied and uncovered.

CHAPTER 11

She Is ... A Scared & Confused Little Girl

"Be daddy's good girl, and don't tell mommy a thing."
"Hell is For Children" by Pat Benatar

AFTER MY MOM AND DAD MARRIED, WE moved to an apartment of our own and he legally adopted me. I have often wondered how it was that I had absolutely no recollection of that day. Knowing how much I loved my dad early in my parents' relationship and how vivid my memories are of the things that happened as the years moved forward, it would have been nice to recall what I have been told was a very happy day.

My uncle moved out and my mom found an apartment for my grandmother and my aunt right around the corner from where we lived. I loved that block. I had more friends than I ever imagined and playing Punch Ball, Stoop Ball, Chinese jump rope, and riding bikes became part of my daily routine.

A short time after we moved in, my grandmother's sister—

Great-Aunt Mickey—also moved onto our block. One of the things my mom loved to do with my grandmother, my great-aunt, and her daughter Ellen was go to bingo. There were several bingo parlors in Brooklyn, plus most of the churches held bingo nights. The women all had their chips, lucky charms, and cigarettes, and they hoped each time they played that it would be the night one of them won the big pot. It was strange having my mom go out without me. Before moving, she never went anywhere without me in tow, even when she played cards with her friends on Friday nights. Now that I had a dad, she could enjoy a few hours with the other ladies in our family.

At first, having my mom go out to bingo was fun. Dad wasn't as strict as my mom and each time she left, he found a way to allow me to do something my mom wouldn't have approved of, had she been home. If I didn't want to eat the spinach I hated, he would allow me to throw it out, making me promise not to tell my mom. "It's our secret, okay? If mom knows, I'll get in trouble." If a show was on that went past my bedtime, Dad would let me stay up the extra half hour, but, "It's our secret, okay?" was the agreement. If he was making us a bowl of ice cream, he'd give me a second scoop and throw extra syrup on it and I always knew, "It's our secret."

He explained that since my mom never had a husband to help her before, she was a little stricter than she needed to be, so we had to keep the secrets because we didn't want her getting angry. He said this is what daddies did; they were fun and let us do the things mommies usually didn't allow. I was simply crazy about him and quickly started to become not only mommy's girl, but his, too.

My dad picked up on the fact that I loved to sing and dance and one of my favorite things to do was listen to records in my room. It wasn't long before he bought me a brand new record player that flashed psychedelic colors on the lid as the records played, and I quickly had what must have been arguably the most extensive record collection of any kid in Brooklyn. They weren't even married a year and already having a daddy was the best thing that ever happened to me.

It was during one of my mom's weekly nights out to bingo that I was sitting on the big gold velvet recliner, watching TV, when my dad called out to me.

"Missy, I need your help. I forgot my washcloth." My dad was taking a bath and as I walked up the hallway, he told me he left it on his bed. I walked into the bedroom but couldn't find it anywhere.

"It's not in here, Daddy."

"Oh. I thought I left it there. I must have forgotten to get one out of the closet." The closet was in the bathroom. "Daddy's covered, so can you just come in and grab one and put it on the side of the tub?"

I walked into the bathroom, opened the closet, grabbed a

washcloth, and closed the door, and as I turned toward the tub, that's when I saw it. It stopped me in my tracks. I couldn't see his face, but I could see him pulling on his private part. It was big and he kept pulling it up and down.

"Did you find one?" I heard his voice, but I kept looking at what he was doing. "Just bring it here and put it on the side of the tub."

I quickly looked down at the floor and did as he said, but I could still see it. As I was walking out of the bathroom, he asked me to do one more thing.

"Don't run off so fast. Talk to Daddy for a while. How was school?" At first I was relieved, because I was no longer actually in the bathroom, but as I turned to lean on the wall outside, I was in direct line with the mirror that hung on the outside of the bathroom door and had the same view as when I was standing in the bathroom. If I switched to the other side of the doorway, I would be looking directly at the tub; either way, I couldn't avoid watching my father play with his privates.

"School was good. Can I go finish watching TV?" I was trying to look at the floor or the wall. I had never seen a boy's privates before and probably wasn't even sure I knew what I was looking at, but I knew it felt like I was doing something wrong and just wanted to go back to the living room and the safety of that velvet recliner.

"Oh, that program will be on again. Talk to Daddy." He

asked a lot of questions and kept the conversation going for what seemed like forever. No matter how hard I tried to avoid looking at it, it seemed like his privates were everywhere my gaze landed. And just when I was sure he would let me leave, I instead saw what would be the first orgasm I ever witnessed. I didn't know what was coming out, but I thought it hurt because I could hear him grunt and breathe heavily. Once he was done, he placed the washcloth over it and allowed me to go back to watching television. But, before I turned to leave he reminded me, "We can't tell Mommy I forgot the washcloth, Missy. She would be angry that you came into the bathroom while Daddy was taking a bath. It's our secret."

That scenario would play out every time my mom went to bingo. And as time went on, each time she went to leave, I would cry and beg her not to go. My mom couldn't understand why it suddenly started upsetting me that she was going to bingo, but my dad was always there to reassure her it was just because she never left me with anyone before and it was something I had to get used to.

Once she was gone, he would go to his room, lie down, and either listen to the radio or watch TV on his small television. He'd still come out and make us ice cream, joke with me, or show me a magic trick, and I'd always wish that would be a night he didn't take a bath. I was confused and didn't know what to do. I believed if I told him I saw him naked, it would embarrass him or make him angry. Would I get spanked or punished for not telling him? Should I have told him to pull the shower curtain down farther? In my mind anything I did was wrong. I felt like I was doing something bad because I couldn't find a way to tell him what I was seeing.

So, I did nothing. When he needed his washcloth or a towel—which was every time—I would run in and only stare at the walls, making sure not to look at the mirror. When he insisted on talking to me, I stood farther away from the bathroom door so I wouldn't see that stuff come out. But more often than not, there was no getting away from the image.

One particular night, my dad took a bath and never called for me. I remember because it was the first time I was relieved that he had his washcloth and towel and I wouldn't have to get them for him. I heard him walk into his bedroom after his bath and he called out to me to make sure I shut the TV and the kitchen light before giving him a kiss goodnight once my show was over. I have no idea how much time was left until the end of what I was watching—it could have been five minutes, it could have been half an hour. I did as I was told and when I walked into the bedroom to kiss my dad goodnight, he was lying on the bed, eyes closed, TV on.

Only as I stepped closer did I see that his pajama bottoms were open and his privates were sticking out of the front hole. I froze. I simply didn't know what to do. Did I kiss him goodnight and leave? Did I just leave him there? What if he was like that when my mom came home? Would he get upset that I didn't wake him and let Mom see him like that? A million thoughts shot through my brain. I decided to just turn off his TV and leave. He'd never know I didn't kiss him and he'd never know I saw his thing.

As I started walking out of the room, I heard his voice.

"Missy? Missy? Is that you? Did you shut the . . . what is this? Oh, God! Missy, did you realize Daddy's pajamas were open? Why didn't you wake me up? Do you know how angry Mom would be if she came home and saw me like this?"

I stood there, frozen in the darkened doorway of his room, and didn't say a word.

"Missy, if you ever come in here and Daddy has fallen asleep with his pajamas open like this, you have to close them. You can't let Mommy see me like this. You know how she feels about us covering up when we're in our pajamas."

"Covering up" was a rule in my home. Pajamas, bathrobe and slippers. No T-shirts or shorts. Nightgowns were acceptable with underwear, but I always had to make sure I was covered when I sat. I understood those rules even at that young age. What I learned years later was that rule was put in place because my mother had been molested at her friend's house during a sleepover. I think about it now, and I realize how easily he manipulated me into thinking it was my fault for not making sure he was "covered."

"I'm sorry, Daddy. I'll make sure you're covered if that ever happens again." I felt guilty and bad.

"Thank you. If Mom ever found out about this or that I let you stay up late or have more ice cream, she would be very mad at us." Clever of him to lump all of them together, no?

My dad never needed my help in the bathroom again. But he did fall asleep again. And the next time he did and I walked into his room to see his penis hanging out of his pajamas, I tried to wake him. He was snoring very loudly like he always did and I shook him so he would wake up.

"Daddy. Daddy! Wake up. I'm going to bed." He woke up briefly and I told him I was going to sleep and he had to cover up.

He said, "Okay, okay," and as soon as I kissed him good-night, he started snoring again. I went back over and started shaking him, but this time he didn't wake up.

I was so scared; I didn't know what to do. I couldn't let him stay there uncovered, and I was afraid my mom was going to walk in the door at any moment.

I shook him a few more times.

He stopped snoring, but never opened his eyes. I didn't know what to do, but I knew I promised I wouldn't let my mom see him uncovered. I took a step back, picked up his private part, put it in his pajamas, and closed the snap. I remember feeling like I had just done something terrible. I remember feeling like I was bad. My dad never moved, never opened his eyes.

The next morning, we were eating breakfast and I couldn't look at him. I was afraid if he knew I touched it, he would yell at me.

"Did you go to sleep right after your show?" He was drinking his tea and eating toast.

"Yes. Shut off the TV and the lights, kissed you goodnight, and went to bed." I couldn't tell him.

"I'm sorry I wasn't awake to say goodnight, kiddo. When you're finished watching cartoons, make sure you help Mom clean the house before you go out to play. And remember, no telling Mom about staying up late. It's our secret, right?"

"Yes, Daddy." Our secret. My secrets.

CHAPTER 12

She Is . . . Enraged & Unhinged

"Go ahead with your own life, leave me alone."
"My Life" by Billy Joel

ONCE KELLY CALLED ME OUT AND MY MEMO-
ries began to flood my mind, I realized it was time to get to
work. I started eating more regularly and a decent sleep sched-
ule was coming together. Kayla was still home from school and
visited almost every day after group. She was taking me to doctor visits and filling them in on my status when I became too
emotional. My anxiety was still through the roof and I knew I
looked as fragile as I felt.

Tessa set up a family meeting. She was surprised when I told
her my mother wasn't going to be included.

"If you want, we can set up a second private, one-to-one
family meeting with your mom," Tessa offered.

"No. No meetings or sessions with my mother. She is off

limits." The thought of sitting in a session with my mother was almost unbearable.

"What's up, Maureen? What are you feeling?" Tessa gently pushed for a better understanding.

"Anyone who learns about my abuse ultimately asks one or more questions: Did your mother know? Aren't you angry with your mother? Do you blame your mother? Do you really believe she had no idea what was going on?" The pain and anger swelled inside.

"My mother lives with the guilt and shame of what happened to me every single day. She's beaten herself up countless times for 'being so stupid,' asked herself aloud, 'How did I not know?' and prayed for forgiveness for allowing that beast into our lives. The only thing my mother is guilty of is falling in love with a man who preyed upon her and her family."

I took a deep breath before continuing. "People want to point fingers at her; they need a scapegoat. They need to believe it happened because someone . . . my mother . . . allowed it to happen. To believe anything less, to be unable to point a finger at her, means that they, too, could be preyed upon. The reaction a large percentage of people have when they learn of this type of abuse is the same as the parent who swears, 'not my child.' They know for sure 'nothing like that would've happened if he were *my* husband.' They're ignorant, frightened know-it-alls. The conversations, hours of crying, and holding onto one another have remained between us and will stay that way. He put her through hell, too. And I know how well I hid it from her."

Tessa just sat there, quietly taking it all in.

"When I finally decided I wasn't going to massage my father or play with his dick and said no, he turned to me and said, 'Really? Well, then I guess this is the end of you. The end of Missy.' I was all of fourteen years old. I swore he was going to grab his gun from the armoire and shoot me dead where I stood. I quickly walked out of the bedroom, went into the bathroom across from my brother's room, and locked the door.

"For almost two hours, I sat on the toilet, listening for my mother's footsteps coming up the staircase as she came home from bingo. And when I heard her, do you know what I did? I waited for her to walk in and lock the door to our apartment behind her, and then I flushed the bowl, unlocked the bathroom door, walked out, yawned, and went back to bed. That's how well I hid it, Tessa. No. I won't put her through it. I won't make her feel she has to explain herself to anyone."

As I spoke I felt like a protective lioness.

"I understand. I won't push for your mom to come for a family session unless you change your mind." I was touched at the compassion in her voice. She never brought up my mother again, but we did decide to do a family session that my brothers, sister-in-law, and Kayla were invited to attend.

I wanted them to get a feel for the clinic and see how it

117

ran. I imagined they had concerns and both of my brothers and Maryann were very receptive and talkative. By the end, they seemed relieved. But Kayla remained quiet. She sat back expressionless, and when Tessa spoke directly to her, she simply shook her head. To have to wrap her mind around the fact that I was so broken was too much. It broke my heart and I worried how this all was going to affect her once she went back to school. It would be several years before I would find out the truth.

After we ended the family session, it was back to group for me.

I was surprised to see Tessa walk into our meeting room. It wasn't too often that she led our group, so it was a nice change. We settled in, went through pulse, and began processing.

"Okay, gang. What's going on? Anyone need to process?" Tessa scanned the room until Bella raised her hand. Bella was a twenty-year-old college student who was fairly new to the program. She'd recently come into our group and was the only member I had a problem with because I didn't believe she was authentic. She seemed more like a a girl who was simply starved for attention and related far too easily to every group member's issue or struggle.

Boss hassling you? So was Bella's. Had suicidal thoughts last night? Bella did, too. Argued with your kids? Bella argued with her parents. Having a manic episode? Bella felt one coming on, as well. There was apparently nothing she hadn't lived through or experienced.

I called bullshit.

"Okay, Bella. What's troubling you?"

Bella didn't answer. She was sitting directly across from me and her whole body was wrapped around itself as she stared at the floor.

Tessa prompted her again. "Bella? What's going on? You raised your hand that you needed to process."

Bella looked up and sighed. "I'm sorry. I just don't really know how to say what I need to without potentially triggering someone."

"Well, if it begins to go in a direction that sounds like it can, I will make sure to guide you. What's happening?" Tessa prodded her gently but firmly.

"Last night, I had a sudden memory of something I forgot. Actually, I don't know if I forgot it or if I didn't remember it happening. I was thinking about the day I did my intake with Delaney and a question she asked. At the time, I answered it honestly—or at least I thought it was honest—and last night I realized I hadn't been honest. But I swear I didn't know that until last night."

Bella was looking almost pleadingly at Tessa, who was waiting for the remainder of her revelation. "I was thinking about what Maureen processed last week . . ." Bella's words snapped

119

me to attention and something deep within began to quietly boil. I glanced over at Tessa, who hadn't broken her gaze on Bella. I switched back to Bella.

". . . how she was explaining what happened to her. I was so sad when I left and deep down, I felt like I could understand what she was feeling and what she went through, but I had no sexual abuse or assault in my history. At least none that I remembered."

I took a long, deep breath. I was biting down on my lips and my leg began to tremble.

"As I was lying in bed, a memory came to me and I realized . . ." Bella picked up her head and looked right at me. ". . . I was also sexually assaulted. I sat up and started to panic. I thought about intake when Delaney asked me if there was any sexual abuse or assault in my history and I said no, but the truth is it is in my history."

Her body pulled in tighter and her head was down. Her shoulders began to move up and down and a small whimper escaped her lips.

"Bella? Bella? Bella!!" Tessa was trying to get control of what seemed to turning into a small breakdown, but all I noticed was that through the whimpers and shakes, not one real tear was being shed. My leg was now vibrating much quicker.

"I'm sorry, Tessa. It's just so much to remember. It happened when I was at school. My boyfriend came over and wanted to have sex. I didn't want to. I told him I didn't want to. We were making out on my bed . . ."

My leg stopped shaking. For the first time, I realized I could be completely wrong about Bella. I was pretty sure I knew where this was going and I wondered just how far Tessa would let her go. We could process in general, but we couldn't give specifics. We could say we were assaulted, but we couldn't give graphic details. There were boundaries. One of our group members found his mother right after she hung herself, but he wasn't allowed to describe what he saw; only that she hung herself, he'd found her, and how he'd felt and reacted. Bella was on such a roll, I wasn't sure how Tessa would stop her, but I braced myself for what I knew she was about to reveal.

". . . and I said no I didn't want to have sex. He kept trying and he kept telling me he wanted me. I didn't want to. I really didn't want to."

My discomfort was growing, but it wasn't because of what Bella was saying. It was from the realization that I had her pegged completely wrong.

He raped her. He forced her to have sex. Those nine words kept rolling through my head like a ticker tape. Here I was thinking all this time she was just a kid who faked mental illness to get everyone's attention, and the reality was she was a victim of sexual assault. I shamed myself mentally for being so self absorbed that I didn't see it. Even her body language—balled up, hands across her chest as if to keep herself protected. Why had I never picked up on it?

I sat on the edge of my seat as if preparing myself to catch the words I knew she was going to say.

"Bella, I have to ask you to be mindful of what you are about to say. We cannot trigger other members. Take a deep breath, collect your thoughts, and then finish." Tessa was very careful to choose her words.

Bella pulled herself together before proceeding. I literally held my breath.

"I didn't want to. We'd already had sex in the past, but that night I didn't want to. I wanted to be held and kissed, but he wouldn't stop asking and trying. And finally after asking, and trying, and asking, and trying . . . I just gave in. After he was done, I felt like I was in a fog. I forgot all about it. I guess I erased it from my memory. But after listening to Maureen yesterday, I realized I had also been sexually assaulted."

Wait. What? What did she say? Did she say she gave in? What the fuck did she just say?

"I . . . I . . . I let him. But I didn't want to! He wouldn't stop asking and trying and I just stopped and let him! I felt disgusting after we finished."

She gave in? She let him?

My leg was now shaking furiously and the ball of rage in my belly was growing so rapidly that I knew I couldn't suppress my anger and sit here quietly another second. I thought she was an attention seeker, but I was wrong. She was a liar and a thief.

I couldn't hold it in.

"So you *let* him and you think that equates to what I shared about my experience yesterday?" I glared at Bella and the words spewed through gritted teeth. "You truly believe that your *choice* to give in and have consensual sex with your boyfriend is the same thing as what I shared yesterday?"

"Maureen, breathe deeply and tell me what's going on inside of you." Tessa was trying to ground me and encourage me to be mindful, but there was nothing but rage.

What was going on inside of me? *She's a fucking liar and a thief, Tessa!* That was what was going on inside of me. She did this all the time. We opened up and shared, and then she could always relate completely to what we were saying. I convinced myself I was a terrible person to doubt her so much. But all along, I was right. What twenty-year-old can relate to everything ten other people are sharing all the time? None!

You are a liar! You consented, Bella! You weren't sexually assaulted or abused. You consented! What you experienced was regret. Girls and women like you are one of the reasons victims *like me are doubted—the reason we keep secrets. You have sex, regret it, then want sympathy. Fuck you, you lying piece of shit! I can't do this! I can't sit here and pretend this is okay!*

"I can't take it. I can't stay here." I jumped off of my chair, stormed out of the room, and headed toward the kitchen, cursing at the top of my lungs.

"Bitch! That lying bitch!" I stomped through the hall screaming until I reached the kitchen. "I finally process and she uses it for her lies. That fucking little bitch!" I was so blinded by anger, I never saw Kelly and Harper at the other end of the room.

"She thinks she can take my life . . . *my life* . . . and use it as a blueprint for her bullshit lies?!!!!" I paced the back wall like a caged animal. No. NO! Not another person who took what was mine without my permission. Please God. Not here! Not in this place, too!

"Maureen. Are you safe? I need to make sure. And I want to make sure you're not going to throw a chair." Kelly was speaking in a calm, soft voice. She and Harper stood in the doorway of the kitchen.

"Am I safe? Yes, I'm safe. Oh, God . . . no, Kelly. I'm not going to throw anything." What the fuck? I was pissed, not suicidal.

"Good. Maureen, can you tell me what's going on? What happened?" Kelly remained calm, cool, and collected.

As I looked at them, I screamed, "Bella! Bella is what happened! Here's some advice: when you're listing all the potential mental illnesses people in here have, pathological liar should be on that list." I was suddenly getting lightheaded and nauseous. I started to cry and sat down against the wall. Both clinicians came to me. "Maureen, what's made you so angry?" Kelly crouched down directly in front of me.

"She tried to compare her giving into her boyfriend's pleas to have sex to what I shared in group yesterday. I finally decided I was ready to deal with the things I came in here swearing I wouldn't talk about, and she takes my story and tries to make it her trauma. She's a manipulative needy liar and does it to gain the attention of the group and the staff. She can have whatever attention she needs, but not with *my life* as her outline."

Now I was the one whimpering.

"She thought it was okay to take my sexual abuse and try to compare it to making a choice to have sex with her boyfriend? It's not! She can't gain sympathy by comparing her decision to what I went through. She chose to give in! I had no choice! It's a painful and ugly story, but it's mine. How could she think it's okay to use my pain to get sympathy? Use my life to get attention for herself?"

"It's not okay, Maureen. And I'm sorry this is how it was received. Would you come into our office so we can discuss it more?" Harper's sweet young face showed such compassion and concern that it brought me to tears.

That rage was a part of me few knew about. It had reared its ugly head only several times in my life. The pain that accompanied it was powerful, unbearable, and came from such raw anguish that when it rose, I believed it would kill me if I didn't release it. But once released, it was uncontrollable and brought to light a side of me I despised.

I stood up. "Sure. I'm sorry I made such a scene. That anger . . . I knew I had to get out of the room."

"I know. It was a moment and you needed space to deal with the emotions that were triggered without people coming from all directions." Kelly offered me a cup of water and I followed them to their office.

I sat by Kelly's desk, sipping water and feeling exhausted. One thought kept looping through my head: "Everyone takes what they want from me without my permission." Another reminder that my life had never been in my control.

CHAPTER 13

She Is . . . Praying

"Because of you, I am afraid."
"Because of You" by Kelly Clarkson

AFTER A WHILE, PUTTING MY FATHER'S DICK in his pajamas wasn't enough. One night when I went to "kiss" him goodnight, he was awake, sitting on the side of his bed watching TV. I again remembered being relieved; no bath, no "covering" him up. Just goodnight.

"Dad's back is really hurting tonight." He winced as he spoke and was trying to rub the bottom of his back.

"Did you hurt it at work today, Daddy?" I sat down next to him. I almost felt happy that he was hurt, but also felt like I was bad for thinking that way.

"Daddy has to climb ladders and some days when I'm installing alarms, my hands are over my head for a long time. I have to twist my body and sometimes it makes my back sore."

My dad installed burglar alarms in banks and other businesses. Mommy made it sound like it was very important work, and dangerous enough that he had to carry a gun.

"That sounds hard to do for a long time. Your arms must get tired." I remembered thinking it was kind of nice that we were talking about his work. Usually when he came home, I was either doing my homework or outside playing. Anything I knew about his job came from overhearing conversations.

I felt like a grownup having him talk to me about where he put in alarms and how he needed to carry a gun in case there was ever a robbery in a bank where he was; it seemed exciting. I was also tired and needed to go to bed, and when I thought the conversation was over, I said goodnight. As I leaned over to kiss him on the cheek, he started to talk again.

"Could you do Daddy a favor? Could you be a big girl and rub Daddy's back? I could really use a nice massage." I didn't have any idea what the word massage meant. "Come up here on the bed. Daddy is going to lie on his stomach and all you have to do is rub down here on Daddy's back, okay?"

He already had his T-shirt off. "I'm just going to lower my pajama pants a little because that's where it really hurts. Don't be embarrassed if you see Daddy's butt. Your butt is really just the top part of your legs, so it's like you'll be rubbing Daddy's back and his legs."

He laid on his stomach and pushed his pajama bottoms

down. His butt was right in front of me and I felt the same way I did when his privates were out. I stood there and started to rub his back with my hands. I was pressing down with four fingers and had no idea what I was doing.

"No, Missy. You have to get on Daddy's back. Just sit on it and put your legs on both sides, as if you were riding a bike." I did as he instructed, but he was a big man and sitting on his back with one leg on each side of him hurt. And, wearing a nightgown with just my panties was very uncomfortable.

"Now, just rub Daddy's back, then slowly work it down toward the top part of my butt." I didn't want to do this; I didn't want to see his ass or touch it. "Yes, just like that. Use your thumbs a little and press hard. Yes. Very good. Take your thumbs and make little circles while you're pressing hard. That will really get into the muscles that are hurting in Daddy's back. Mmmm . . . yes, baby, just like that. Talk to Daddy. Tell me all about your day."

I remembered my little mind racing.

I don't like this. I don't want to talk. I don't like Daddy's voice. It doesn't sound like him. I don't want to touch his butt. Do all daughters touch their daddy's butts like this? My mommy doesn't even let me see her in her bra. She would never let me touch her butt. I want to go to my room. I want Mommy to come home.

I talked to him about my day and kept rubbing his back and his butt. Then very suddenly and very quickly, he told me

I'd done a good job, and that I should get off his back and go to bed. As I climbed down, he asked me to hand him the tissues on the side of the bed and when I did I saw his belly was wet.

"Thank you, baby. Daddy feels so much better. Mommy doesn't like to give massages, but now I have you. This stays between me and you. We don't want to make Mommy upset, okay? There are a lot of things Mommy doesn't understand because she never had a daddy, so there was no one there to explain things to her." I remembered just standing in front of him as he wiped his belly with the tissues.

"Yes, Daddy. I know. I won't say anything to Mommy." She would be so mad at me.

"Good girl. Give me a kiss goodnight. I love you."

What is that smell? I feel sick. I don't want to say I love you.

"I love you too, Daddy."

I don't love this daddy. I love the one who is here when Mommy is home. But the daddy who is with me when she is at bingo is someone I don't like. I don't like how he makes me feel. I don't like what he makes me do. And, I don't like this smell.

I crawled into bed and looked outside my window at the church across the street. I said my prayers, but felt bad when I didn't want to ask God to bless my daddy.

He makes mommy happy. He married my mommy and now we live in a really pretty apartment. He does magic tricks. He lets me stay up late. I have to ask God to bless him! He has a dangerous job. What if I don't ask God to bless him and while he's working in a bank, some robbers come in and kill him? Would that be my fault because I didn't keep him in my prayers? What if he died tomorrow and Mommy asked me if I kept him in my prayers and I told her I didn't? It would be my fault. She would never forgive me because that would be why he died.

"God bless Mommy, Grandma, Aunt Kathy, Uncle Jimmy, Grandma, Grandpa, Uncle Danny . . . and Daddy."

CHAPTER 14

She Is . . . Fed Up

"I wanna be the one in control."
"Control" by Janet Jackson

IT HAD BEEN A WHILE SINCE I'D HAD SUCH A
sleepless night. The rage I felt about what Bella did, the memories it stirred up, had sent my mind racing. Once again, I was
exhausted but couldn't fall asleep. I felt like my life had been the
longest-running boxing match and I still didn't know how to
protect myself from the knockout punches. I understood that
no one had the perfect life, but at what point was it okay to ask
God for a do-over?

I dragged myself into Forward Moving after managing to
squeeze in four hours of sleep and ran smack into Tessa.

"Good morning. Got a sec?" I hadn't seen her since storm-
ing out of yesterday's group and I was in no mood to have a
bright and happy bullshit chat. I sat down next to her desk as

she shut the door. I reminded myself I was not angry with Tessa and took a deep breath.

"You didn't stop in before you left yesterday." The sentence just hung in the air. I remembered that, yes, Tessa told me she wanted to talk to me about something before the earth swallowed me up momentarily.

"I forgot you told me you wanted to meet with me, Tessa. I just wanted to get home, have a cup of tea, and go to bed. I had a lot on my mind." Like wanting to rip Bella's head off.

"Mmm-hmm. Yesterday was very interesting. I wasn't quite sure why you reacted that way toward Bella. What's going on?"

I'm pissed, Tessa. And did I mention I want to rip Bella's head off?

"She's a liar and she craves attention, Tessa. She listens and watches us work our asses off, then comes in the next day and finds a way to suddenly relate to exactly what we spoke about." Now I was annoyed with Tessa.

"Isn't that what you're here for? To be able to listen to other people share their experiences so you find some comfort, knowing you aren't the only person struggling or feeling the way you do? Doesn't sitting in a room with others who have gone through similar experiences give you the ability to share?" Everything Tessa said sounded reasonable. But when it came to Bella, I knew I wasn't wrong.

"Yes it is. But we have to be truthful about what we are

struggling with in order to support each other. She isn't being truthful, Tessa. She's using our experiences and twisting them to suit herself. Why is she even here? Does anyone know? Has she ever truly shared herself with the group?" My anger was rising.

"So you're angry because you believe she's a liar." Tessa looked at me with a knowing expression, but she had no idea.

"No, Tessa. I'm angry because she *is* a liar and she wants sympathy for something that didn't happen. She believes if she acts pathetic enough, she can convince us that her consent to have sex with her boyfriend was actually sexual assault when it wasn't."

"But your reaction still doesn't add up, Maureen." Tessa was pushing harder than she realized and my anger was stirring.

"How doesn't it add up, Tessa? She lied. Girls like her invalidate girls and women like me who have actually experienced sexual abuse, assault, and rape. She is someone who makes all of us look like liars and why people don't believe us and question us. Girls like her are the reason guys who rape get away with it. *She* perpetuates the mindset that women ask for it or yell rape when they regret a bad choice. Does it add up now?" Internally, my body was shaking.

"Stop a minute. Women like you who have experienced sexual abuse, assault, *and* rape?" The shaking stopped. I'd said it. I'd said that word.

RAPE.

I was eighteen years old. I was dating my first serious boy-friend. We went to Junior High School together but didn't start dating until I was almost sixteen. He was a year older than me, and I fell head over heels in love with him. He was the first boy I had sex with, and I was sure it was forever.

Until he started cheating.

Until he started getting rough with me.

Until one day after a fight he threw me down on my bed and raped me.

I'd never told a soul. And, I hadn't revealed it on my intake form when I came to Forward Moving.

"So Bella has triggered more than you've shared." As I looked at Tessa I felt panicked. The thoughts running through my head were too much, and I found myself wanting to fall back on one of my oldest coping skills.

When I was four, the house I lived in with my mother, grandmother, Aunt Kathy and Uncle Jimmy caught on fire. Again, my memories were snapshots.

I hear firetrucks wailing up the street as I'm playing in the front yard.

I put my hands over my ears.

A firefighter grabs me from the front yard and runs me across the street to hand me over to someone I don't know.

I'm screaming. In my confusion I'm afraid this stranger is going to throw me in the fire.

As more firetrucks pull up, I again throw my hands over my ears screaming, "NO! NO! I don't want to get thrown into the fire!"

My grandmother and uncle are pulled out of the house.

My mother is running from the corner after getting off of the train.

I watch my mother run toward our house.

"NO! NO!" I scream again, hands over my ears.

We were lucky none of us was injured or died. Both my grandmother and uncle were unconscious, but would recover. My mother was stopped from running into the house and found me with the stranger who was actually a neighbor I didn't know. But, from that day on anytime I heard a firetruck I instantly put my hands over my ears. And, when I became overwhelmed or unable to cope with any kind of fear or stress, covering my ears—even if it was with a shrugged shoulder—remained my automatic response.

The memories of the rape and my childhood made me want to sit there with my hands over my ears. I didn't want to face the fact that I wasn't capable of continuing to pack my past in a neatly wrapped box. But, I also understood I was here to heal and covering my ears would not help me get to where I wanted to be.

Instead, I chose to use some of the skills I'd been taught and was practicing. I grounded myself and breathed deeply. I wanted to get better. I had to do the work.

"Yes, Bella triggered a lot more." *Too much to sit here and re-hash.* "I have been in this group for a while now. It's a safe place to come and a place where I don't feel like I have to apologize for what I think or how I feel. But regret is not rape."

A sense of pride washed over me as I came to the realization that I had faced my anger, tamed it and was not afraid to speak with complete honesty.

"For anyone to believe it's okay to take what I shared and manipulate it and distort it to gain attention is wrong. Do I resent her feeling vulnerable or unable to find the confidence to say no to something she didn't really want to do? Absolutely not. Do I resent her for possibly feeling like she doesn't fit in or doesn't feel attractive? No.

"But she's mistaken if she believes the only way to get comfort and support from me was to lie about experiencing the same trauma I have endured over years. The only response that would ever get is anger and getting called out for being an attention-seeking shameless liar."

Tessa sat quietly and let me continue.

"I'm tired of people taking from me without even asking.

I came here to deal with my shit. I came here to undo, or at least learn to accept, the damage other people did to me. I've never asked anyone for anything. All I've ever wanted was to be happy. HAPPY. At no point in my life have I done anything so terrible that I should have to work so hard for so long to simply feel normal."

I caught the emotion that was suddenly welling up inside. I'd desperately prayed for as long as I could remember to simply be given the opportunity to wake up without having to put up my dukes and fight someone or something every single day.

"I've made myself bounce up and move on so many times, but this last round felt like I met my match, and I almost gave up. I often wonder how many more hits my soul can absorb before it dies? I don't speak of these thoughts; I accept the hits and take three months off from my life just to relearn how to function again like a normal human being. And what do I get? Some attention-seeking little girl who thinks it's okay to hone in on my life story. It's a shitty, nasty, disgusting, nauseating story and if someone wants it they can have it, but they have to live it first."

Was I angry? Yes, but more than that, I was tired. I was hurt.

"If you try to take something of mine without my permission, you're going to get the full wrath of those emotions, and I don't give a shit who likes it or not."

Tessa stared at me with no expression. I didn't care. I was

not apologetic for what I'd done or how I felt, and for once the universe was going to have to deal with it.

"Well then, okay. If that is how you feel, then the timing couldn't be better." An image of Scooby Doo flashed in my head as he said, "Rut Ro?" Was I going to be discharged? Did she think I was okay to end treatment?

Tessa continued, "The powers that be were tossing around the idea of starting a Trauma track for quite some time, and approval came through a little over a month ago. I was asked to spearhead the program, and have finished the training. I want you to be one of the first members, Maureen. I have two other patients who will be asked, but I think it will be the perfect setting for you to practice the tools and coping skills you have been given to regain control of your life. What do you think?"

Not what I'd expected as a response, but I was so relieved, I didn't have to think twice. It had taken weeks, but I knew things were starting to shift, and I knew my clinicians had given me the best chance to walk out of there whole again.

"Yes. I would love to help you get the program off the ground." The entire time I'd been here, I was the only person to experience sexual trauma. "Will there be other members who have the same history as I do?"

"Not initially. But the other two patients have also experienced life-altering traumas. There are emotional and psychological similarities in all trauma victims. You will all be able to relate to the emotions you struggle with due to those traumas." I could see Tessa was excited about this new track, and I felt like it was another new beginning.

"Three of us, huh? Three of us in a 45-minute session as opposed to seven or eight of us means more time to talk, less chance to hide. This should be interesting." I gave Tessa a knowing smirk.

She laughed. "It's groundbreaking, Maureen. There is no other program like this in New Jersey. We're learning so much about how trauma affects the brain and how people react to triggers they aren't even aware exist. I'm happy you're angry. Beneath all the sadness was where that anger lived. It's the anger that's been eating away at you. I know you're afraid of it. I know you didn't like how it made you feel. But I told you at some point you would learn how to exist in your discomfort without making reactionary decisions. Trauma track is where you will continue to learn those skills."

I was excited. I was scared. I knew this was my chance to live the second half of my life happier and more in control than I'd done for the first half of my life. There was a tremendous amount of openness and freedom that came with having nothing to lose. Tessa explained that I would no longer be a member of the groups I'd been in and it made me sad. I'd gotten to know everyone, care for, and trust them. Somehow we'd become a family, but I also knew I'd done all the work I could with them and it was time to move on.

All aboard the Trauma track.

CHAPTER 15

She Is . . . That Type of Girl

"My monsters are real, and they're trained how to kill."
"Monsters" by Shinedown

AS TIME PASSED, MY FATHER'S REQUESTS FOR massages began to include giving them, too. Having him rub my body and touch me always made me feel sick in my stomach.

"This will help you relax. Remember what I told you about your butt really just being the top of your legs. That's all that the lower half of your body is. Your belly ends and your legs begin. People try to make it dirty and it's not." I wondered if all dads and daughters did these things. I thought about the dads who lived on my block and didn't believe they would say and do these things with my friends. I was uncomfortable and my body became something my dad touched whenever he wanted. It didn't belong to me.

Some nights I would pretend to fall asleep on the chair in the living room and he would come in to shut the TV, then quickly send me to bed. When he thought I was sound asleep, he would come into my room, sit on my bed, and stroke my hair, telling me how much he loved me. Sometimes he'd rub my back or my butt under my pajamas. I wouldn't move and would breathe very quietly. I stopped crying when my mom went to bingo; it did no good and started to make my dad angry.

When my brother Christopher was born, and again after my brother Bobby was born, things stopped because my mom wasn't going to bingo as often and even when she did, my dad was busy feeding, changing, and putting them to sleep. I thought that because the three of us shared a room, my dad would at least stop coming in when he thought I was asleep. But eventually, things started all over again.

I was getting older and my mom and I had the birds and the bees talk. Now I knew what my dad was doing was wrong. People were only supposed to touch each other like that when they were married. My mother explained the difference between good girls and bad girls.

I began to believe I was a very bad girl.

My escape was being outside as much as I could to see my friends. 84th Street was a safe block and I could be a normal kid. I was well-liked, athletic, and popular. Being out of my house felt safer than being in my house.

But again, all of that changed in an instant, and the idea of anything ever feeling safe began to crumble.

By fifth grade, I started maturing physically. I had boobs, a waistline, and an impressive set of long legs. At twelve, I could easily pass for fourteen or fifteen, and I realized even the boys were starting to treat me and the other girls on the block differently. Spin the Bottle, RCK (Run, Catch, Kiss), and Seven Minutes in Heaven took the place of Tag, Punchball, and Stoopball, but it was all part of us starting to grow up and even those games remained innocent.

Having two younger brothers meant my mom needed a little more help and my responsibilities in and around the house increased. Several times a week, my mother would ask me to run up to the corner grocer, and pick up milk and bread. It was a rite of passage I looked forward to, and it made me feel grown up and important. It required crossing a busy street; walking there by myself proved my mother trusted me to be responsible. My reward for going to the store was always a Kit Kat bar and sometimes being able to keep the change.

I had been going to the grocer by myself for several months. The owner knew my routine, and each time I walked in the store he would take a Kit Kat, hold it up, and put it to the side for when I was ready to pay. Most of the time there were one or two other people in the store, just standing at the front counter or right outside the door talking. One afternoon, I walked into the store and headed toward the back to grab a gallon of milk like I had every time before. The store was empty and the owner was in the back loading the shelves instead of at the counter as he usually was. I quickly said hello when I saw him, and as I opened the door was startled as he said hello back to me because he was suddenly standing right behind me.

I glanced up, smiled, then turned to grab the milk. As I stepped back to let the refrigerator door close, he hugged me from behind.

I froze.

He leaned in.

He was talking in my ear, telling me what a nice girl I was. I just stood there, still frozen, holding the milk. I said thank you as my gaze moved up and I looked in the reflection of the refrigerator door. His hands began to wander up my shirt and he was rubbing my breasts. Then he took one of his hands and shoved it into my pants and started rubbing me between my legs.

"You such a nice girl. So pretty. You always so nice." His breath was hot and he smelled stale.

I stood there holding onto the milk, staring up at us in the reflection. I could see the cars driving by, hear the train pulling into the station. It was a beautiful day and I watched through the reflection as people walked by. *Can't anyone see us? Please! Someone? Anyone?*

I prayed someone would walk in.

No one did.

"You like the candy. I have candy in back. You come later and I give you all the candy you want. You come back? You take candy, okay?" I knew if I came back he would do something worse, but if I said no I thought he would drag me all the way into the back and kill me.

I promised I would come back before he closed. He stopped touching me, let me go, then followed me as I walked to the register. He went behind the counter and was smiling.

"You take two candy now. You a good girl. You come back later and get all the candy, okay?" He came out from behind the counter and put his sweaty hands on my shoulders. "You come back. I see you later and give you all the candy." Again, I promised I would, and managed a smile as I walked out the door.

I stepped out into the sunlight, crossed the street, and, when I knew I was out of his sight, threw the Kit Kat bars in the street. I was twelve years old. Two men had felt my breasts. Two men had touched my body. I hated my body. I felt disgusting and embarrassed, but I knew I could never tell anyone. If my mom knew, she would be angry. If my friends found out, they wouldn't like me anymore because I was one of "those" girls; the type of girl that allowed men to touch her.

I never went back to that store. I wouldn't eat a Kit Kat again for years.

After that day, anytime my mom sent me to the store, I

would run the extra two blocks to Frank's Deli to get milk and bread, then run back until I was a few houses away and I could walk. I didn't have permission to go to Frank's because it was under the "L" and that avenue was very busy and too dangerous for me to cross. I was already a liar. I was old enough to understand that the "secrets" between me and my dad were lies. Now I was becoming a sneak.

I stopped going out to play with my friends. My block and my neighborhood didn't feel safe to me anymore, and I started spending more time with two girls I went to school with and going to their houses. I drifted from my friends on 84th Street and in less than a year, we moved from that four-room apartment to a six-room apartment several blocks away. I missed my friends; I missed being a part of something. But I didn't feel like them anymore.

Things were happening to me no one would ever understand. My dad had been abusing me on bingo nights for years and started to get more brazen. He would press himself up against me when my mom was in another room as I washed dishes or folded laundry. He would pull my shirt away from my body and look down at my breasts. If I pulled away, he would grab a breast and tell me, "I'm just playing around with you. Stop being so sensitive." He'd laugh and wink, then press up against me one more time before he walked out of the kitchen.

Men had the power to do whatever they wanted to me.

CHAPTER 16

She Is . . . A Phoenix

"All we need, all we need is hope."
"Rise Up" by Andra Day

THE FIRST WEEK OF BEING ON THE TRAUMA track had me rethinking my decision. With me, Jenna, and a gentleman named Art as the only members in the room, the "group" element was sorely lacking. That quickly changed the second week, when Pete and Kim were brought in to be a part of the Trauma group. Pete, a high school math teacher and Kim, a stay-at-home mom, were part of groups on other tracks and switched over to this group due to their traumas. Kim was desperate to share every part of her trauma while Pete was quiet and seemingly unwilling to share anything about himself. Although I would never wish this type of trauma on anyone, I felt relieved to finally not be the only person coping with sexual assault and abuse.

Jenna and Art didn't remain in the group for very long. They were at the end of their treatment time and graduated out of the program. A graduation ceremony consisted of only the members who were part of your main group and the clinician running it. The clinician would ask the group to call out positive affirmations and one group member would write the words on a board, while another wrote them on your graduation certificate.

I wasn't crazy about graduations. Twice a day we were part of bigger groups that discussed health and self-care topics. We met a lot of other patients outside of our main group who were not invited to participate in our graduation. And, when graduation happened to coincide with new members being added to your main group, graduation was uncomfortable. The new patients didn't know who the graduate was, or what they'd accomplished so they really couldn't contribute. By the time we graduated, most of us had done three months worth of hard work. In my mind, our departures should have been celebrated on a larger scale with everyone inside and outside of our main group.

Graduation aside, it didn't take long for Trauma to feel like home to me. I'd finally found my tribe! And, as a founding member of the group, I felt like it was my responsibility to work twice as hard to make the new track successful. As I listened to what the group members shared, I felt more like myself each day. I was changing and could measure how far I had come as new members were brought into the group.

I became a motivator, cheerleader, and group mom.

My sense of humor and easy laughter returned. I was applying the coping skills I'd learned early on, and became the group member who encouraged new members to work the program, and assured everyone that what we were being taught was invaluable and worked. Because I felt safe and understood in this group, I shared and spoke easily. I was sleeping better and eating again. When I looked in the mirror, I no longer saw the shell of the person who'd entered the program. I could see myself and, even more importantly, my family saw that I'd turned the corner.

My goal was to be not only the best graduate to ever leave here, but to be an example to the others that our hard work would pay off. And, when they became doubtful, I always reminded them how brave they were to commit themselves to healing and that we were all forces of nature.

I was already stepping down. I started at five days a week, came into the Trauma track at four days a week, and was now down to three days a week. Graduation was looming, and I wanted to help the new patients coming in get acclimated to the program, and be the fellow group member to put their mind at ease.

But on that day, I would be reminded that there was still

work to be done. As much as I enjoyed being a motivating presence, I was here to help myself most of all.

As we settled in for our meeting, the mood in the room was light. Kim had finally reached a point where she didn't feel the need to vomit every fear into every meeting, and had herself become a very positive presence. She had endured sexual abuse from her husband and the guilt of finding out he'd also sexually abused their adopted sons. Her world was rocked to the core and I sometimes felt as if we were witnessing her nervous breakdown unfold in front of our eyes.

Pete came in the complete opposite. He didn't want to share his trauma. He spent many meetings looking down at the floor, trying to disappear. I adored him the second I laid eyes on him because I could see he was such a gentle soul. The day he revealed he had been raped by a stranger as a child and had lived his entire life never telling anyone, I openly wept. The shame, confusion, and pain he revealed were familiar, but still so heartbreaking.

Looking at him sitting across from me, laughing and chatting easily, I felt as if I was witnessing breakthrough after breakthrough. I was so honored to be a part of this world and to watch the broken pieces of so many souls being put back together.

We've been battered, abused, and left powerless. We lived with shame and guilt. We kept our secrets and the secrets of those who brutalized us, and simply tried to move on. The moment the weight brought us to our knees, the moment we broke, we felt weak and alone and at some point truly wanted to die.

We all walked in praying to find a way to be the people we could have been and wanted to be, and here we are, smiling and hopeful. We were brought face to face with our wounds and secrets, and once spoken, began to believe they no longer possessed the power they once had over our lives. It's the moment we pray for. It's the moment we never think will come.

That day, however, we would begin to understand that facing our pain didn't fully erase our internal narratives and that everything we had been taught, everything we'd been expected to practice, would be put to the ultimate test.

Tessa presented the group with a simple question that required a one-word answer.

"If I were to ask you to describe your core belief of who you truly are in just one word, what would that word be?" Tessa scanned the room for the first word.

"Survivor." Amanda was a fairly new member of our group. She was young, beautiful, and endured the worst side of college life. She had to be brought home and landed here with us. I loved her spirit and wanted her to succeed, but my first thought when she said the word was "bullshit."

More words like resilient, fighter, and strong filled the room, and each time, "bullshit" jumped into my head. I sat in my seat not saying a sound. I knew exactly what she was asking the group. They didn't understand what Tessa meant by their core belief.

I did.

She wanted us to say the word that defined us. For some it'd been a lifetime, for some less, but we all had that one word we'd never spoken. The word that, if anyone knew or heard it, would reveal our vulnerability. My word, my core belief popped right into my head, but to say it out loud? No. I couldn't.

To say it out loud would mean everything I had experienced shaped me.

To say it out loud meant I hadn't been able to simply move on in my life.

To say it out loud meant every part of the life I'd tried to build was actually a façade . . . a lie.

To say the word out loud meant I was acknowledging my ugliness, my stupidity, the hurt and pain I'd caused others, and my failure to create the life I so desperately wanted.

To say the word meant more work had to be done and perhaps I wasn't the group leader I portrayed.

To say the word meant I was a fraud.

I looked up at Tessa and realized she was staring at me. She understood the impact that question was going to have on me. There was no softness, no "You can do this" behind her gaze. There was just an unspoken understanding that this was a part of my treatment that was unavoidable. This was what stood between my climbing over my wall of fear or remaining stuck behind it. This exercise was for me to take over today.

No cheering on the others in the room.

No motivating another member to say what they feared.

This was my moment. With this exercise, Tessa was silently saying to me, *"Your time here is limited. Time to step up and show the group what it is to be a leader, that there is always work to be done, and be unafraid to show your vulnerability. Time to prove to yourself that you, too, are a force of nature."*

"Maureen? What is your word?"

I hadn't felt this way in several weeks. Internally, I was pleading again. Pleading for her to not make me do this. "Tessa—"

"What's the word, Maureen?" Tessa cut me off. "I know you don't want to. But you also know you can't continue to give it the power it has had over you your entire life."

I sat a few seconds and then just said it.

"Worthless. I'm worthless. I've always been worthless." As I said it the third time, I began to sob and decided not to try to stuff it back in. I'd been working up to that since I got here. I'd been working up to that for forty-two years, and I'd finally found a place to say it.

"Go on. Explain why that is your core belief." I'd explained it to Tessa early on, but never to a group.

"I had a good life before my mother married. I don't remember ever thinking or questioning why I didn't have a father. My uncle lived with us and he was the only male figure in the house. He was protective of me. He took me to nursery school and played with me when he was home. I guess he filled the role of a dad."

I was happy. Life was perfect.

"When my mother met my father and they fell in love, I was excited. I fell in love with him, too. He was handsome, funny, and made me feel safe and loved in the beginning, much like my uncle did. But once my father started abusing me, once he told me the truth about my mother having me out of wedlock and that my real father walked away from us, my belief became that I should be grateful for my father, and whatever love he showed me. It wasn't a conscious decision. It just became my prevailing thought."

I should be grateful. Some girls didn't have a father.

"My uncle married and had his own family. I didn't see a lot of him except at family gatherings and occasional visits. He loved me as much as he always had, but now my father was the man in my life. He was in charge. He was responsible for me now. He was the one I answered to. So I felt I should be grateful. And at least I had a dad who made my mom happy. At least I had a dad who put a roof over my head. At least I had a dad who put good food on the table. At least I could say I had a dad like everyone else."

These thoughts. These words. They are the narrative I have lived my life believing. They are the "truths" on which my breakdown is based upon.

"In the words of my great aunt—the woman my mother adored and looked up to her entire life, the woman who showed my teenage mother how to be a mom—my father 'gave me a name.' Why couldn't I simply push aside what happened, forgive and forget it? To my family, *HE* was worthy; *HE* earned a pass for making me legitimate. Whatever hurt came with it was what I had to swallow. I was a mistake. My mother sacrificed a promising future because of me. She was going to be the "success" in the family. I brought nothing but pain and shame to the table from the moment I was conceived. I was worthless and my father was the hero, no matter what he did behind closed doors."

He was our savior. His behavior made me believe other men also had permission to do whatever they wanted to me. I wasn't good enough to be respected by any man.

"As I got older, that feeling of worthlessness grew without me even realizing it. Boys and men who wanted me made me acceptable in my eyes. How they treated me behind closed doors didn't matter. I was willing to do whatever they wanted in order to repay them . . . thank them . . . for the privilege of being chosen. Having a man in my life told the world I was worthy of being loved, of being someone's partner. Without them, I was worthless. Without them I was a girl, a woman, no one wanted. I needed a man to make me legitimate in every aspect of my life."

Every other girl was the girl guys brought home to Mom and Dad.

"And the badder and tougher they were, the better. In my mind, they protected me from other men trying to hurt me. I was one of those 'bad' girls, after all; one of those girls all men just wanted to touch. Being with a man who was connected or simply a tough guy meant no one would ever touch me. I was *their* 'good girl.' And if they weren't the nicest guy all the time, or were controlling, it was okay because no one else would fuck with me as long as I was their girl. And when the relationship ended, that prevailing thought: 'I'll never be worthy of a man's love' would choke me. I was nothing without a man."

Scream at me, smack me, grab me, even rape me . . . just don't leave me. Leaving me is the worst thing anyone can do to me. Leaving me left me vulnerable to the unknown; not knowing who would come and try to abuse me or, worse, if anyone would ever want me again.

"A core belief is who you truly believe you are but will never reveal to anyone. It uncovers your vulnerability. And the few times you thought you found someone you could reveal it to, they just used it to hurt you. Survivor? Strong? Resilient? Those aren't the core beliefs of anyone in this room. They may be how we hope to see ourselves, but they're far from core beliefs."

I finally took a breath.

It seemed like all of the light and life had been sucked from the room. The air was deafeningly quiet. I'd just blown to pieces all their validating words. Now they got it. Now they understood the question.

I cried as I drove home. Those feelings, those truths had eaten me up alive and although I knew uncovering and releasing them were critical, speaking the words was unbearable. Here I was, day in and day out, working harder than I ever had, but each time I managed to stand up without holding on and take a few steps, I knocked myself back down.

"How was your day?" I'd been living with my brother Chris, my sister-in-law Maryann, and my niece Emily since my breakdown. Maryann had been a godsend. She greeted me every morning with a hug and an "I love you," a cup of tea, a shoulder to cry on if I needed it, and an ear to listen if I wanted to talk. And when I didn't want to talk, her smile and her hugs were the constant reassurances that I was surrounded by people who loved me and were rooting for me.

"Oh, Mare . . . every time I start to feel good, like I'm making headway, one of the clinicians throws an anvil in my direction and knocks the wind out of me."

"I can't say I know, but I can tell how far you've come. Chris and I have been so relieved to see you get better every week. I feel like my sister-in-law—the one I met so many years ago—is finally back. You've been gone for so long." Maryann looked so sad.

"I haven't been gone that long. My breakdown was only a few months ago, Mare." I laughed as I said it, but she still looked like she'd lost her best friend.

"It hasn't been a few months, Maureen. It's been years. It started right after your first Valentine's Day. I remember."

Our first Valentine's Day was the first time I'd sensed something was wrong, that CJ may not be happy. We were together ten months, but he was growing distant. He booked a reservation at the Liberty House restaurant. It was a beautiful place that looked right across at the New York City skyline. I was so excited, but he was preoccupied.

When we sat down, it was obvious he was troubled, but every time I asked if he was okay or if something was bothering him, he just kept telling me he was tired, that all was well. It wasn't. I realized much later on that was the beginning of his relationship with Michelle.

"It's been five years, Maureen. Five years of watching you disappear little by little." Maryann's eyes were tearing up. "I've hated him for a long time. And Chris can't stand him, hasn't liked him for years. We put up with him for you. We didn't want to lose you and we knew if we made you choose, we would never see you, so we smiled through gritted teeth. But we could see something was terribly wrong. I look at you now and cry, but it's because I'm so happy and so grateful you're back. My laughing, smiling, crazy sister. I've missed you, both of your brothers have missed you, everyone who loves you has missed you." We were both crying as we hugged. I'd put my family through hell.

"I had no idea, Mare." I was stunned.

"We love you and never wanted to risk losing you. But bit by bit, we all watched you disappear. No more bursting through the door with your big smiles and hugs, less and less of the laugh we all love, less joking around, less visits. And even when you were with us, just the way he spoke to you, made jokes at your expense, ordered you around, and ignored you? You were always trying to please him just so he wouldn't lose his temper in front of us, but we saw it; we felt it."

I was dying on the inside. My family was going through hell and I was blind. I was so caught up in my own chaos, I couldn't see what they were going through because of me.

"I'm sorry, Mare. Sorry for everything. Sorry for not listening when you all told me it was too soon to move in with him, sorry for bringing him into all of our lives, sorry for pulling away. I'm so ashamed." I hugged her tight, hoping she felt every ounce of love and gratitude I had for her and my family.

"Don't be. Just continue getting better. The last time we

were together with you and CJ, I think all of us knew something terrible was going on. I told your brother I was so afraid something was going to happen. But that is all in the past because you left. It doesn't matter to me what or how long it took. You finally left."

CHAPTER 17

She Is . . . Almost Silenced

"But my words, like silent raindrops fell . . ."
"The Sound of Silence" by Simon and Garfunkel

WHEN MARYANN MENTIONED THE LAST TIME we were all together, a familiar ache settled into the pit of my stomach. I was Humpty Dumpty that day, only I didn't have a wall to fall from; CJ smashed that wall so hard, it exploded and I didn't just break, I shattered.

My brothers and their families were going on the *Polar Express*, a holiday train ride event. With Kayla away at college and things with CJ unraveling, I thought it would be fun to be with my nieces and nephews and that maybe being in a festive environment would get CJ off of my back.

When I looked at it now, I didn't know what I was thinking or hoping for that day. CJ's verbal abuse was almost daily and I realized now I had given up. I was numb to it. I suspected he was cheating on me with Michelle again—if it had ever really ended—but leaving seemed impossible. The money I made at my job wasn't enough to cover rent in my own place and CJ spent his money at will. Whenever he ran out, he just asked me to "loan" him what he needed and when I didn't have it to give, he interrogated me. It crossed my mind several times through-out the years that CJ had a gambling problem, but asking or hinting at it would have just been denied, or worse. I lived my life simply doing what I had to do to keep him from getting angry.

Our relationship made me feel trapped, which was exactly how I felt growing up with my father. Hearing his car pull into the driveway brought on the same dread that hearing my father walking up the stairs did. The tone in CJ's voice when he would call "Maureen!" was the same as when my father would call for me. But far worse than his anger was his cruelty. When he started using the things I feared or that brought back terrible memories, my home became my cage.

When I was a kid, my father forbade me to lock the bathroom door, saying, "What if something happens to you? What if you fell and hit your head? I couldn't get to you quick enough." If I was showering or going to the bathroom on the nights my mother went to bingo, my father would simply burst in and ask why I was taking so long. There was never a knock. As I matured and locked the bathroom door in "defiance," my father would scream at me to open the door. When I refused, he would peep through a space between the door and molding, and watch me go to the bathroom or undress before showering and drying off after showering.

When CJ and I first moved in together, I would lock the bathroom door. He asked me why I locked it, and when I told him he promised he would never walk in on me without knocking. CJ's response was kind and gentle, and he seemed sympathetic. "What kind of sick human being does that to their daughter or any woman, for that matter?" He made me feel so safe and was so understanding that to prove I trusted him, I stopped locking the bathroom door. But, it only took a couple of weeks before CJ thought of a way to push that envelope.

He would knock at first and ask if he could get in to brush his teeth while I was in the shower, and I never objected. But after three or four times, as he brushed his teeth, he would ask me if he could peek over the curtain to take a look. I told myself he cared enough to ask, that this was normal for couples, and I let him.

He was gaining my trust.

"You know if I had the time I'd join you. I love watching you soap up." He'd tell me he loved me, then leave for work. Each time he knocked, he'd ask if he could get his morning peek, then he'd kiss me and go. It made me a little uncomfortable—I never liked my body—but I felt lucky he found me so desirable.

The first time he didn't knock, I never even heard him come into the bathroom. All I heard was the curtain being thrown completely back.

"Surprise!"

I shrieked and grabbed the curtain. "Jesus, CJ! You scared me half to death!" It felt as if every nerve in my body froze.

He just stood there laughing.

"Oh, stop. I'm just playing. I'll call you later." As he walked out the front door I could still hear him laughing. I told myself I should be thankful he was attracted to me and wanted to admire my body. But, from that day on he stopped knocking on the door altogether. I always felt so exposed and vulnerable. And when I tried to ask him to stop coming in for a peek without knocking, he turned it around.

"Oh, c'mon, Maureen! All normal couples play this way; peek in on each other. Stop making me feel like I'm a pervert. I'm not your father. Don't blame me for your daddy issues." I was so ashamed, felt so guilty for making him feel like he was doing something wrong that I apologized. He continued doing it, and although it made my skin crawl every time he did, I pretended it didn't bother me.

It wasn't long before CJ pushed the envelope as far as he could and barged into the bathroom all the time, even as I was on the toilet. I was mortified, but I kept trying to tell myself it wasn't a big deal. But, as things went downhill and he became physically abusive, I started locking the door. He would twist and turn the handle, pounding away on the door as he screamed at the top of his lungs.

"Open this fucking door, Maureen! Trust me, I have no desire to see your fat, disgusting ass!" Eventually he would kick or punch the door and stomp away as he called me a stupid bitch, ugly mole-faced witch or something equally hurtful.

On the day of our family outing, CJ started off in a great mood. I was relieved because not only were my brothers and their families going, my mother and two of my cousins and their families were also joining us. We drove my car because there was a chance of light snow and CJ's car drove terribly in the snow. He seemed excited to be getting together with my brothers and their families for a bite to eat, then meeting up with the rest of the family for the *Polar Express*.

We drove up Route 18 and stopped at a convenience store to pick up coffee, tea, and a snack for the ride. After getting back into the car, CJ went to back up and another car came into the lot, driving faster than he should have, and jumped into a spot several cars away from us. CJ honked the horn, but the guy got out of his car and ran into the convenience store. CJ was furious.

"That f'ing jerk off! He almost hit me! Driving 100 miles an hour into a parking lot!" His great mood was over.

"I'm sure he didn't mean it. He's probably just in a rush. C'mon, sweetie. Let's just get back on the road. It's gonna be a great day." *Oh God, please let's get on the road.*

"Nah. We're gonna sit here till he gets into his car. Motherfucker is gonna learn not to speed through a parking lot, almost hit me, and ignore it." CJ was already spiraling. When he got like this, it was as if his face, his voice, everything about him changed on a dime.

"CJ, please. We're going to be late. We don't know what traffic will be like. Screw him, he's an idiot. He didn't hit us, so let's just go and eat." I was careful to put in the "screw him" so CJ wouldn't accuse me of siding with the other driver.

"Relax! Just shut up and let me handle this, Maureen."

This day is already over before it has even had a chance to begin.

We sat with the car running as CJ stared at the side view mirror and I remained in the passenger seat, checking over my shoulder. Finally, the guy came out and jumped into his car. As he pulled out of his spot and started driving toward the exit, CJ quickly backed up, then slammed on the brake. I thought my neck snapped.

"CJ! What are you doing?" Before I could finish the question, CJ was already yelling out of his window.

"You don't see me pulling out, asshole?" CJ was screaming as the guy rolled down his own window and bellowed back at him.

"Why don't you look when you're pulling out, you stupid prick?"

All I could think was, "No, no, no. Don't yell back at him. Don't curse him." I was starting to panic.

"CJ, please stop! Just stop!" I couldn't stand it. Couldn't stand the scene he was making. Couldn't stand his outbursts. Couldn't stand being afraid every single time we went out that he was going to find someone new to bully or say something nasty to. It was too much.

"Shut the fuck up, Maureen!" CJ was gripping the steering wheel. "I'm handling this. Jesus Christ!"

As I looked over at him, he opened the door and charged the other guy's car. Without missing a beat, the other guy climbed out of his car, too. This was everything I always feared whenever CJ and I went anywhere—that one day, his size and big mouth wouldn't be enough to scare someone away. That one day, his cutting someone off in anger, flipping them off as he screamed, "FUCK YOU!" and chasing them down a highway to scare them would backfire, and the tables would turn.

I could hear them screaming and threatening each other, but I couldn't move, couldn't turn around. It was as if something inside of me broke; like I accepted that whatever was going to happen would happen, even if it meant the other guy was a lunatic that was going to kill both of us. I sat there listening to their argument, threats and taunts of "C'mon! Do it! Come at me! I'll kick your fucking ass!"

People coming out of the other stores stopped and stared. I was trapped in this car, panic-stricken with no way out. I thought about just getting out of the car and walking away. I thought about calling the police. I thought about being anywhere but that parking lot.

I closed my eyes, and put my hands over my ears.

What was only minutes felt like hours until CJ finally jumped back in the car.

"Ugly ass douchebag and his loudmouth cow of a wife!" He loved this; loved escalating anything he saw as a sign of disrespect so that he could bully and badger people. I didn't move. The day had started out with such promise and it was already ruined.

The other car went to go around us, but CJ cut them off to get to the exit first.

"You're an asshole!" the driver's wife screamed out of the window.

"Screw you and your pussy husband, you fat c**t!" CJ roared back at her as he sped onto Route 18, laughing like a madman who had just lost his mind.

I just sat there, staring out the window.

"Can you believe them? Assholes, both of them." I didn't respond. "Motherfucker thought he was a tough guy. And his ugly ass wife, thinking if she got out of the car it would make a difference." I didn't even look at him.

"Hey! What's the matter with you? Oh, now I'm gonna get the silent treatment from you? Now you're gonna ignore me?" I had been in this situation a thousand times before. I knew there was no winning. Staying quiet was the safest bet. We hit a red light.

"No answer? I'll tell you this much; at least his ugly cow of a wife gave a shit and had her husband's back. You just left me out there like a dick. Didn't give a damn about what happened to me. And now you're just gonna give me the silent treatment? Yeah, you love me. Right. Nothing to say? No smart answers for me now, huh? Answer me, Maureen, or I swear to God I'll kick you out of this car, right here!" CJ was screaming at me like a madman. I finally spoke.

"You're gonna kick me out? Out of *my* car, then drive away? Do it. Please try it, CJ. Before you get to the next light, I'll call it in as a stolen car. I want to go home." I spoke so quietly. I was falling apart internally and half expected him to grab me or move over to my seat and scream into my ear like he had many times in the past. I knew I couldn't go to the *Polar Express*; there was no way I could fake being excited and happy after what just happened.

"Home? Nah. We're not going home. We're going to the *Polar Express.* I'm not gonna let you ruin this day for me. We've had this planned for weeks and now you just want to go home? And what are you gonna tell your family? What a prick I am? Talk shit about me? I'm not letting you do this to me. We're going. Fuck you!"

For the rest of the hour-long trip, I didn't say a word. CJ continued to berate me and blame me for being a drama queen, for not having his back.

When we got to the restaurant to meet my brothers and their families before the train ride, I put on my happy face, but CJ's rage couldn't be hidden. He barely spoke to anyone, even the kids, and when we returned to the car to drive over to the train, he continued to berate and curse me for ruining his meal. The rest of my family—my cousins and their families, my aunt, and my mother—were meeting us at the station and the dread inside of me was growing rapidly. I had to do something to calm him down so my family wouldn't feel his rage.

As we walked down the path to the train, I swallowed my pride and turned to him.

"I'm sorry, CJ. You're right." I choked on the words. "I shouldn't have ignored you in the car and I'm sorry I ruined lunch. Can we please start over?" He wouldn't look at me. "Please, CJ. The kids are so excited you're here. My whole family is excited we're joining them." I reached up and kissed him.

"I don't know why you have to do this to me, Maureen. That jerk off was wrong . . . wrong! And you ignore me and treat me like I'm the bad guy? Unfucking real. Nah. You decided it was okay to disrespect me and now you want to make it all okay? No problem. I'm good." He was looking over the top of my head, refusing to look at my face. I could see my mom waving us over and the empty pit in my stomach was growing. I knew what I had to do.

"You're right, CJ. I had no right to do that to you. I was just scared and didn't know what to do. I should have trusted you had it handled." Please, please God, help me salvage something of this day. "I shouldn't have disrespected you. He could have hit us and was completely wrong. So was I. I should have gotten out of the car as soon as his wife got involved. I'm sorry, babe."

"When are you going to learn, Maureen? I know how to handle my shit! I tell you all the time to relax, I got it covered, but you think you know better. I'm glad you realize this never had to go this far. You need to stop being such a drama queen." I wanted to scream. I wanted to tell him, "NO! You're wrong! You're nuts!" but I couldn't. I had to diffuse that now.

"I will, CJ. I'm sorry. I just want us to have fun, okay? Can we just hold hands and get on the train with everyone and have a great time?" I leaned up and kissed him again. I was so ashamed because I didn't want to kiss him. I wanted him to go away. I wanted to go on the train without him, but I couldn't allow this to go on.

"You blow everything out of proportion, Maureen. You just don't learn. You have to get me all wound up and ruin half the day before you realize what you're doing." He was playing the martyr. He did it so well that even I began to believe I was the problem. "Yeah, okay. Let's go." I went to grab his hand, but he pulled it away. He'd determined to keep this going without letting anyone else know, but I didn't care. As long as he could put on a good face, we could get through this day. CJ hugged my mom and started playing with the kids. He was strategically ignoring me but I didn't care.

"Everything all right?" my mother asked as she hugged me.

"Everything is great. This is going to be so much fun." I was trying to get back in gear, but even I noticed that I couldn't seem to find the tone or emotion I was trying to project.

As we sat in our seats and the train pulled out, I felt nothing. No happiness, no anger, no excitement or joy. I was sitting with my family feeling like an observer with a frozen smile on my face. CJ was playing with the kids, the *Polar Express* characters are performing, my family was singing and laughing. It was the perfect picture. But I was simply an observer.

I sat next to my mother and I noticed she hadn't let go of my hand. She kept looking over at me and rubbing my hand at the same time. She could sense something was terribly wrong and the guilt ate away at me. I didn't want her to worry. I wanted to laugh and sing and be the silly, carefree aunt I loved being to my nieces and nephew. I tried, but I couldn't find her. I watched my brothers and their families, how happy they were in this moment. It was bittersweet because I was so happy for their happiness, but at the same time I realized I'd never know the love they shared.

I chose a man who took pleasure in berating me and pushing me down, but once I'd realized who he really was, it was too late. After five years, I was simply too tired to fight back. Too embarrassed for my loved ones to find out what I'd tolerated. Too fearful to admit how much power I gave up because I loved him. Afraid I would look weak if I shared with them how it went from wonderful to awful.

I wanted to look at my mom and plead with her, plead with my family, "Please get me away from him. Please help me," but I was too ashamed. I'd taken the blame in order to calm him down and given him more ammunition to use against me. How did things deteriorate to this level? God, I was so tired.

Two days later, I woke up in silence.

CHAPTER 18

She Is . . . Finally Grieving

"You can't hurt me now . . ."
"Oh Father" by Madonna

WHEN I LOOKED BACK ON THAT MORNING, I finally understood that my breakdown was inevitable. I'd lived in denial most of my life. Telling myself I was a failure as a daughter, mother, wife, and girlfriend was more bearable than facing the lies and betrayals I experienced as a child. Hiding the truth was easier than allowing myself to grieve for everything that was taken—everything that could never be replaced.

My breakdown was the grief I wouldn't allow myself to face, but had to release. I needed to grieve for that little girl. I had to allow myself to grieve all the hugs, kisses, moments of pride, and adoration she looked forward to that were replaced with confusion, shame, and fear. I needed to grieve for the little girl she was before that man came into her life; the girl who saw the world through innocent eyes, and had hopes and dreams. That girl would never know the love a daddy has for his daughter, would never be any daddy's little girl.

Giving myself permission to finally face the reality of my life also meant grieving for the teenager and young woman who never believed she had any value. She . . . I . . . would never get a do-over.

Finally, I had to face that by choosing CJ, I'd chosen a man who was exactly like my father. They were bookends, and I'd ended up trapped on both sides.

Allowing myself to grieve would bring to the surface so much pain I feared it would kill me. But continuing to push it down, to deny that grief most assuredly would. I had been slowly dying my entire life, and for one brief moment waking up in silence felt comforting.

Thankfully, I heard the sound of silence and realized I had to turn up the volume.

You walked into her life one day
So funny, handsome, and tall
The moment your hug lifted her off the ground
In love with you she did fall

The smile you brought to her mommy's face
Never before had she seen
Her mommy looked at you like you were a king

PRESS PAUSE

About to make her his queen

The day you did, the little girl learned
She would also become your daughter
And couldn't wait to show the world
She now had a her very own father

Before that day she didn't know
All the fun she had been missing,
Sitting on daddy's lap, getting big bear hugs,
And watching her mom and dad kissing

How special she felt you had chosen them
Like unwrapping a present each day
She couldn't have known it wouldn't last
Her daddy would soon go away

Now in his place a stranger appeared
And never again would she see
The tall handsome man who had been her dad
Gave big hugs, and had sit on his knee

He looked the same, and said the same things
To her mommy he'd said before
But what no one knew was the stranger who appeared

SHE IS . . . FINALLY GRIEVING

When Mommy walked out of the door

"You're special, you're my girl, I love you so much . . .
Mommy would never understand,
The special love I feel just for you
Would just make Mommy very mad."

"If Mommy knew, she'd cry and be sad,
And it is my true belief
She'd pack up my bags, put them out the front door,
And tell me I had to leave."

"Once again you and Mommy would have to move in
With your aunt, uncle, and grandma
And never again would you get to see me,
Your new grandma, or new grandpa."

So the little girl promised, though it didn't feel right
To keep the secret for her dad
She believed if she told, again her mom would be alone
And always and forever be sad

She wished on stars, promised God every night
If her daddy returned she'd be the best girl
But, he never did, it was the stranger who stayed,

And upside down he would turn her world

As the years went on, a young woman she became,
Their secrets she still did keep
But the stranger she knew could no longer stay
A secret hidden so deep

No more hugging Mom, no more kissing Mom,
No more love for her mom in his eyes
He was now a stranger to both, and the young girl could see
Her mom's beautiful brown eyes pleading "Why?"

And so the day came when the girl made the choice
To tell her mom the truth and reason why
The man they both loved had left many years before,
And she'd also been living the lie

Her mom sat there in disbelief,
Learning all in her life that ever mattered
The man she loved, the family they built,
Was all built on lies and now shattered

It took many years
But the girl, her brothers and mom held each other tight
And rebuilt their family, knowing their bond and their love

SHE IS . . . FINALLY GRIEVING

Had turned such a wrong so right

As time passed and their family grew
One night as they sat in their homes
They each received a call the stranger passed away
Sitting in a hospital wheelchair all alone

The woman who once had been that young girl
Sat frozen, silent and still
Always wanting to hear the apology she hoped for
Realizing now she never will

"I'm sorry I hurt you, you did nothing wrong
You were the best daughter a dad could have;
It was never your fault, and every day of my life
I have wished I could take it all back."

"Instead of being the best example
Of how a good man should treat you
I made you believe you were dirty and unworthy
A pain I can never undo."

After finally learning to come to terms with my past
With support from those here and above
No longer do I feel dirty, broken or unworthy

PRESS PAUSE

And I have created a life I love

Finally believing I am strong and worthy
A work in progress, I continue to heal
Smiling and laughing, looking forward every day
To the gifts my life has yet to reveal

CHAPTER 19

She Is . . . Worthy

"I believe what you say of me."
"You Say" by Lauren Daigle

MOST OF THE DAYS SPENT IN TRAUMA HAD been devoted to acknowledging the places within ourselves that no one liked to visit, then reminding us how to use our coping skills to stop ourselves from reacting automatically and getting lost in our ruminations. When I first entered the program, I resisted practicing those skills. Telling myself to simply stop thinking by picturing a stop sign and distracting myself with something else seemed ridiculous. It couldn't be that easy, and I said as much in group one day.

"I can't grasp the thought-stopping exercise. Just picture a stop sign or tell myself to stop, then move on to another activity? How can that possibly work? The thoughts that run through my head feel like they're on a loop, as if they're obsessive compulsive. It's just not that simple."

Margaret sat next to me. As I spoke, in a way that clearly indicated I thought it was a ridiculous idea, she suddenly jumped out of her seat, stood directly in front of me, and screamed, "STOP!" right in my face. She scared the shit out of me. "The next time you can't stop your thoughts, think of me as your stop sign. Remember me yelling STOP! in your face." I sat there stunned as she sat back down, but the next time I tried it, it worked.

I was sitting in Trauma telling that story to a new member in our group when Kelly walked in and said, "Tessa, we're in the big room. Let's bring everyone together."

Tessa asked us to move to the big room. We were combining with another group, which never happened before. As we walked in, Kelly was sitting in the front with the "torch bearer." We sat on the floor and in a couple of the empty chairs as we joined the other group. The facility had a tradition in which they named a patient the Torch Bearer. That was someone who put 100% into working the program, a patient others looked up to and was a leader.

A patient who followed through with everything they were asked to do and who stood out because of their commitment to healing and encouraging their group members to do the same. When a Torch Bearer was named, they quite literally passed a rubber Statue of Liberty torch over to him or her and the new torch bearer wrote their name on it alongside all those who came before them. The torch was theirs to carry or keep at home until it was time for them to leave and the clinicians chose a new patient to carry the torch.

We all sat there like children waiting to hear who would be named class president. To anyone who wasn't in the program, it would probably seem childish. But to those of us who understood what it took to take time off from your life to rebuild yourself from the inside out, to talk about things that were unspeakable, for those with addictions to work their asses off to maintain their sobriety, for those who suffered with mental illness to learn how to take care of themselves, it was an acknowledgement from the staff of how far you had come and that you stood out among your peers. It meant you were regaining control and creating a new life for yourself.

Quite simply, it was an honor.

"As you are all aware, our current Torch Bearer is almost ready to graduate, so we had to pick someone to carry on the tradition. For the staff, the choice was unanimous. Our new Torch Bearer not only stands out to the clinicians, but to every patient who gets to know her. She has completely transformed since her first day here and has become a true leader to everyone in her group. I think all of you will agree there was no other choice. So please give a hand to our newest Torch Bearer . . .

Maureen." Kelly sat there like a proud mom. And as I looked over at Tessa, her smile was bigger than ever before.

I was stunned. As Kelly called me up to take the torch, I was overwhelmed by the applause and cheering in the room. It felt as if everyone knew it was going to be me and they agreed with the clinicians' choice. Up to that moment, I had experienced many moments of joy and pride, particularly as a mom. But this was the first moment I felt joy and pride for something positive I had done for myself, and it felt great.

Kelly hugged me. "We were all in total agreement. You possess all the traits we look for in a torch bearer. You show up early every day, you work hard and follow the program, you are supportive to everyone in your group, and you have a great attitude. I'm so proud and so happy for you."

"I don't even know what to say," I told her. I signed my name on the torch and began to cry.

"Can you share a little bit of what the last couple of months have been like and have taught you for the new members who are just starting?" I looked at Kelly's face and it hit me that that moment wasn't just an acknowledgment of my growth and hard work, it also signified success for the clinicians. The Torch Bearer wasn't just for those of us struggling and actually beginning to see the light at the end of the tunnel. The Torch Bearers were tangible proof that what our clinicians were doing made a difference. We were their success as well as our own and I was suddenly aware that the silly-looking torch carried a lot of weight and value. That torch represented a life saved, a life changed.

As I looked across the room, I spotted a few familiar faces, but not because I passed them in the hallway or saw them during our lunch break. Their faces were familiar because they were me the first few weeks after starting the program. The blank stares, body hugging positions, and overall sense of despair they wore were what I had shed while doing this work. I chose my words carefully.

"I was a shell of a person the day I arrived. All I could ask myself was, 'How the hell did I end up here?' I wanted to go back home, go back to bed, and never wake up. I was mentally and emotionally exhausted, felt ashamed and guilty for what I was putting my family through, and wanted to die. After being greeted by Tessa and given the introductory tour, I noticed a sign hanging by the door that said, '90% of your success is just showing up.' I thought it was bullshit. I thought the coping exercises they spoke about were bullshit. I thought this place was bullshit. Success meant having something to show, whether it meant a happy marriage and family, a high-paying job, vacations, or money. I had none of those things, so in my mind, I was a failure on every level.

"But I was wrong. I started to realize showing up meant to show up for me, for life, and to engage in it. It didn't mean there wouldn't be hardships, sadness, frustration, and worry. The sign simply meant to show up, keep the promise I made to be the best version of myself I could be, and be present in my life every day. I wasn't doing my best up to that point. I was smug and convinced this place had nothing to offer. But I realized I knew nothing about how to get my life back because if I did, I wouldn't have had to be here. Nothing else up to that point in my life worked, so I decided to give it everything I had.

"Almost three months later, I don't even recognize the woman who walked in here. I have the tools I need to handle my trauma and its aftermath. For the first time in my life, I know I can take care of me, and that is what it means to show up. My advice, even though we're not supposed to give it? Listen to them. Put everything you have into the program, because it's for you."

Tessa was grinning from ear to ear. "See what happens when you show up?"

I grasped the torch in my hands. "Life happens when you show up." I couldn't stop crying or smiling.

As I drove home, I called Kayla and my mother. After explaining what it meant to be the Torch Bearer, they both shrieked and told me how proud they were of me. They'd had front row seats to my breakdown. They'd held me, wiped my tears, worried endlessly about me. It felt so good to give them some kind of proof that I was healing. When I got home, I shared the news with my brother and sister-in-law, who were equally excited. I hadn't felt this good in such a long time. This was finally the break in the clouds that had hovered over my head for so long, and it felt fabulous.

When I went to bed, I had a moment when I considered how CJ would have responded to my funny-looking torch. I had cried endless tears for weeks over leaving him. I lost thirty pounds in almost two months and hours of sleep that I would never get back. What would he have said? How merciless would he have been as he made fun of me? And just like that, I told myself to STOP! I pictured Margaret's face in mine. I went back to my daughter's voice, my family's excitement, and fell asleep feeling proud.

CHAPTER 20

She Is . . . Prepared

"Shoot me down, but I won't fall. I am Titanium."
"Titanium" by Sia

TESSA AND I SAT IN HER OFFICE. I HAD BEEN the Torch Bearer for three weeks and graduation was a day away. Being the Torch Bearer seemed to shift my relationship with Tessa, Kelly, and some of the staff members. The conversation became friendlier and I learned more about them and their lives. I knew we weren't forming a friendship because it was against the rules, but somehow I felt a part of their circle. Tessa and I were going over my aftercare strategy and I suddenly felt very emotional.

"I know there are people who can't wait to get out of here and those who are afraid to leave. I'm just sad as hell that I won't be seeing all of you anymore." The rule was that once a patient left the program, clinicians were not allowed to engage in any type of friendship for three years. If a former patient was in crisis and needed assistance finding help, they could call their program clinician, but beyond that there was to be no contact.

"You're going to be fine, Maureen. It's normal to feel nervous, it's normal to feel sad, it's normal to feel like you wanna run out of here." Tessa laughed at her own remark and I thought back to the first time we met. I wanted to scream at her after she told me it was normal to feel nervous that day. I caught the cry that was suddenly stuck in my throat and covered it with a big smile. "Every patient's reaction to graduation is different. We will miss you, too. But I'm confident you won't be someone we see again and that's all I could ask for. I told you once that you were a warrior with a fragile soul. You still have no idea what a miracle you are, Maureen. The fact that you were still standing when you walked in here spoke volumes about your strength. You are worthy of everything good that comes your way. You always have been. I hope you never forget your worth and if you do, you have the skills to put you back on course."

Some of the patients have had to repeat the program several times. They either didn't follow their aftercare strategy or left too soon due to limitations set by their health insurance. Most, however, just never believed in the program and were sent back after being hospitalized. I was touched by Tessa's confidence that I was a patient who was going to be successful.

"It will take time to feel worthy, Tessa. I can't lie. But I do know now that I deserve more than what I have accepted, and I never want to go back to that dark place."

"I'll take it!" Tessa clasped her hands together.

"You want to hug me, don't you? I know you want to hug me. And I know I'm your favorite." Tessa was not a warm and fuzzy woman. In fact, there were moments when I wondered if she truly enjoyed being a clinician. She didn't hide her impatience when members weren't following the rules or were eating up a group session by sharing their uncondensed version of what had them anxious. But I appreciated our conversations and the relationship we had built. Her ability to keep her distance forced me to face painful truths without having her to hide behind.

"I'll hug you on the way out. Tomorrow!" And with that, Tessa excused me from her office.

I headed home and tried to get to bed early, but to no avail. The nearly three months I had spent working on my traumas after walking through the doors of Forward Moving, simply wanting to die, had been life-changing. Although I was nervous about being less than twelve hours from having my safety net cut loose, I understood that what I accomplished was monumental on a personal level. I was engaging in my life again, seeing friends, enjoying my family, and releasing old unhealthy habits while embracing healthier, positive habits.

As I sat with my thoughts, my mind drifted to CJ. Our

break wasn't as cut and dry as I'd led the rest of the world to believe. While in Forward Moving, CJ still found ways to get to me. He left CDs of our favorite songs on my windshield, cards professing his regret, and text messages and emails begging me to give him another chance. Without my family's knowledge, very early on in my treatment, I gave in and met him at the reservoir.

As soon as I saw him, I burst into tears. I sobbed so hard I could barely speak and all he could do was hug me. Once I regained my composure, we walked and talked, cried and hugged. He told me over and over how much he loved me and would wait for me to get well. It was as if it never crossed his mind that he was a big part of why I became so sick. It never dawned on him that he was the straw that broke the camel's back. As we said good-bye, CJ told me to make sure I did what I needed to get better, and remember how much I meant to him.

We spoke sporadically, but as I got further into the program, I realized I could live a happier life away from CJ. As hard as it was to believe, I knew I still loved him and missed what we had in the beginning of our relationship. I still needed to believe there was good in him. I still told myself that his past wasn't any more normal than mine on certain levels and if he worked hard enough, he could change. I even suggested he think about going to Forward Moving for himself and he said he would. I quietly prayed that he meant it. Despite the abuse, I felt sorry for him and continued to hope he would give himself a chance to be helped.

I reflected upon my family, especially my daughter, and what I'd put them through. In the past, I would have allowed the guilt and shame to cripple me. Instead, I felt the pain, allowed it to wash over me, and then decided that rebuilding my relationships with all of them so they would again see me as a strong woman would be my mission. I was going to have to accept that their anxiety and fear about me breaking down once more wasn't going to end because I graduated. It was my responsibility now to prove through my actions that they would never again have to worry. I must regain their trust and show them that I could handle whatever the future held and conquer it.

CHAPTER 21

She Is . . . On Her Way

"Look at me, I'm coming back again."
"I'm Still Standing" by Elton John

"SO . . . HOW ARE YOU FEELING?" I WAS SITTING at the kitchen table, looking out the back window and having a cup of tea when my sister-in-law sat across from me. "Are you sad or ready to move on?"

Sometimes it felt as if Maryann and I truly were sisters. She knew I was not happy because she realized what being a part of this program meant to all of us. She understood how close I had gotten to Tessa and Kelly, and she understood how much of an adjustment it would be not to see them every week. They took me in at my very worst, and were now sending me off as the best I'd ever been.

"I'm a little bit of both, with a healthy dose of fear," I admitted. "I'm going to wake up next Monday and back to work

I go. I have been so disconnected from the world and I guess I'm just wondering how long it will take me to feel like I fit in again. I will miss everyone terribly, but the work is done." I was sad, but I was also proud. That first day, I wanted to run back to my brother's house, lock the door behind me, and never go out into the world. Everything was painful; everything made me cry; everything was a reminder of what a failure I was. I didn't want to smile or laugh or go out or fall in love ever again. I just wanted to remain within the safety of my family.

Looking back, my heart broke for that person. The pain, the betrayals, and the guilt I carried? I didn't know how I didn't break sooner. Now there was nothing in front of me but endless possibilities to be happy and comfortable with who I was.

"I would feel the same way. But you worked so hard and are again the person we all missed so much. I wish I could be there with you." No one was permitted at graduations due to HIPPA rules. Only the patients in your last group could attend.

"Me, too. I wish you could all be there." I glanced at the clock. "Gotta go. I'll see you when I get home." I hugged Mary-ann tightly. "I couldn't have done this without you all, but especially you and Chris. Giving me a roof over my head that afforded me the time I needed to get back on my feet is something I can never repay."

"Family doesn't keep a running tab, Maureen. I love you."

She embraced me again and twenty minutes later, I walked into the facility for the last time.

Each group I visited that day said their good-byes. Each group leader had something inspiring or a piece of advice to send me off with until I was finally with my last group. Tessa was our leader and I could already feel myself getting emotional as I waited for our meeting to begin.

"I made these for you." Pete, who was an incredible baker, made his famous almond caramel chocolate cookies for my graduation. I hugged him tight and immediately stole one. "They will be in the kitchen for you to share, then take home."

"Thank you, my sweet friend." Pete was the first man I'd ever known who admitted to being abused. Out of everyone in our trauma group, he was my favorite group member because of his sweet and kind disposition.

"All right everyone, we have some business to get through and then we can begin Maureen's graduation." Tessa jumped right in to make sure there wasn't anyone who needed to process, and then Kelly walked in, calling her out of the room. When Tessa returned, she looked stressed.

"I'm sorry, guys. The powers that be need this room pronto." She let out a very annoyed sigh. As we began to pack up to move, Tessa stopped me. "I'm sorry. You know we can't rush processing, but I'll get through it as quickly as possible, especially now that we have to move rooms. I don't want to rush your graduation."

I followed her down the hall, telling her, "Don't worry about it. Life happens, but now I have the skills to deal with it."

"Yes! That is the truth." I smiled broadly as Tessa opened the door and I was stopped in my tracks. The room was filled with everyone from my groups and every clinician and staff member I had worked with over the three months I had been there. I turned to Tessa, confused for a moment.

"What is this?" Everyone began to laugh and clap as Tessa leaned over to answer my question.

"Everyone wanted to say good-bye, Maureen. We made the decision to combine all the groups for the last meeting. The staff, the patients, and even Delaney wanted to send you off. We meant it when we told you that you are a warrior and you proved it to everyone here."

There was a chair in the middle of the room that Kelly asked me to sit in. As I took a seat, Margaret went up to the board to prepare to write the words that those in attendance would call out to describe who they believed I was, while another patient took my certificate to write the list so I would always have it. I looked up at the board and there were two words at the top.

She Is . . .

"As you can see by the amount of people who wanted to be here, you have made a huge impact on so many since you arrived three months ago. The staff has quite literally watched you fight for your life and in doing so, you have been an example of determination and healing to all. No one wanted to miss the opportunity to wish you well and say good-bye." Kelly told me later that it was the first graduation in all the time she'd been at the facility that the exception to allow so many to attend one graduation had been granted.

The ceremony began with the clinicians recapping my first day and my journey to graduation. I wish I could say I remembered what they said, but I was so overwhelmed, I simply sat and cried.

As Tessa wrapped it up, she turned to Margaret, who stood at the board. "Okay. Let's begin. Margaret, start us off with a word you feel describes Maureen.

"True friend." Margaret wrote it, and immediately the others joined in.

"Helpful!"

"Determined!"

"Beautiful!"

"Resilient!"

"Fearless!"

"Kindhearted!"

"Capable!"

"Wise!"

"Hysterical!"

The list grew longer and longer, and as every word was added, I repeated it in my head. "She is strong."

"She is comforting."

"She is fierce."

"She is unique."

The list seemed endless and I silently promised to live up to every single one and accept the beauty of how other people saw me.

"Torchbearer!"

"Sweet!"

"Force of nature!" I laughed at that one because that was the phrase I'd used many times to remind others in my groups how strong they were to have endured their own traumas.

"Intelligent!"

"Great Mom!"

"Authentic!"

On and on, the words kept coming until it almost seemed as if there were no more to share.

"One is missing. The most important one." Kelly was sitting on the side of the room and she and Tessa were smiling from ear to ear. "Worthy. She is worthy."

In that moment, my mind tumbled back to day one, to the first time I shared, the first time I cried, the first time I showed up to a meeting wearing a color other than black every day, the first time I laughed, the first time I exploded, the first time I realized I was becoming who I wanted to be and was meant to be, the first time I realized how important it was to simply show up.

"Is there anything you would like to say, Maureen, especially to those in the room who are still fairly new to our program?" Kelly finally offered me the opportunity. I looked around the room and knew exactly what I wanted to say.

"I hated this place when I started. I hated the staff, the patients, the fact that I had to be here at all. But the thing I hated the most was my life and myself. I hated my past, the things I experienced, the mistakes I made. I had no joy, no life, no future to work toward. And I had no faith that anyone here would change my opinion. But the truth of the matter was, if I had the answers, if I knew how to find all the things I lost, I wouldn't have needed to be here.

"So after just showing up the first few weeks, I promised to work the program. I promised to do whatever I was told. I let go and allowed the clinicians to take the lead. They didn't lead me back to who I was, but led me to exactly who I was supposed to be all along. They gave me the opportunity to feel and face my emotions in order to see myself in ways I had never experienced. They allowed me to find hope and showed me how to deal with the emotions and triggers that will always pop up from time to time. They taught me that I could be afraid and still be in control. They taught me to trust myself, my instincts, and my decisions.

"When you hate this place, and I promise you that you will, remind yourself that it's the only place that will allow you to begin again. It's the place where you will actually be introduced to yourself and experience the first day of the life you were meant to live all along."

My nervous breakdown saved my life.

It forced me to press the pause button and begin again.

EPILOGUE

Because She Is . . . Ready to Press Play

I WAS FIFTEEN YEARS OLD WHEN I REVEALED to my mother what was going on. Looking back, I believe that may have been the first time I started to break down. I got up, put my school uniform on, and caught the bus. But, my body and my mind weren't connected, and I moved about emotionless. My father's little games of grabbing me, looking down my shirt, punishing me, and keeping me from my friends were taking its toll on me.

I went from being grateful for having a roof over my head, clothes on my back, and food on the table to dreaming about being able to get a full-time job and leave. I couldn't wait to leave that hell I was in. I went to a gifted and talented school, and my grades were good enough that I skipped eighth grade. I was going to graduate right after my seventeenth birthday. That would give me a year to save money and move out when I turned eighteen. I had it all planned out. But, the closer I got to eighteen, the further away it seemed. And I just couldn't hold it in any longer.

I was beginning to give up hope of ever having a normal life.

So, I arrived at school, walked to my locker and just stood there staring at it. The girls were arriving, locker doors slammed, students talked and laughed, but I just stared at my locker.

I can't be here today was the only thought I remember having before I turned around and walked right out of the building. I walked the twenty-four blocks and arrived at Aunt Kathy's apartment. As I knocked, I prayed she would be home.

She was.

After letting me in, I sat at her little kitchen table and finally allowed the dam to break and the pain to pour out of me. As I shook and cried, I told my aunt every detail of what my father had been doing for nine years. Guttural cries and moans escaped, and sobbing so intense I had to stop and catch my breath. To this day it was a pain for which I have no words.

Once I revealed the truth, Aunt Kathy picked up the phone and told my mother she was stopping by. She then called her cousin Ellen who lived around the corner and told her to go to my house, too. Aunt Kathy then instructed me to stay put until she called me to come home.

Two hours later, I got the call.

As I walked into my apartment and into the kitchen, I could see the pain and confusion on my mother's face. As she looked at me with her tear stained face, I froze.

"I'm sorry. I just didn't know how to tell you." I wasn't just apologizing for the bomb I'd laid in front of her, but because I told others our business. I exposed our dirty laundry, and put our shame in the spotlight.

"You are going to live with Aunt Mickey, and when your father comes home he is going to the VA hospital to get medical treatment." I was packed and sent off before the day ended, and my father was admitted the next morning.

Aunt Mickey only lived two blocks away, but I might as well have been in another country. It felt so far from home. I wasn't in my bed. I wasn't with my brothers. I wasn't with my mom.

I told.

I couldn't keep the secret, and now my family was broken apart. My brothers were only five and eight years old, and because of me, their father and sister were gone. My mother was left alone to try to pick up the pieces. Her sister didn't speak to her for months. She didn't go by her house. Once again I felt I'd changed the course of her life, and permanently extinguished the bright light that lived behind her magnificent brown eyes.

But the light wasn't extinguished forever.

The bond my mother and I share is unbreakable. She is

my rock and I am still her precious girl. And time healed the relationship between my mom and her sister. What I thought destroyed us, what I thought broke my family into a million pieces, actually made us stronger, closer, more open. More secrets were revealed, allowing for more healing to happen. And our family's legacy was changed. That doesn't mean we don't still sometimes have our struggles, too. We are just more open about them.

Throughout my childhood and into my late teenage years, I held tightly to the belief that God would reward me. Surely, all the abuse, pain, and secrets I kept to protect others would ensure a happy, fulfilling, easier future, wouldn't it? God couldn't possibly expect one child to survive so much, only to bring more pain and grief into adulthood, right?

In a perfect world, perhaps.

What I have to accept is that there's never a moment anyone wakes up and suddenly discovers their life has become easier or simpler because they'd been dealt a shitty hand.

I would love to write that after leaving Forward Moving, I was able to build a quiet and uneventful existence, that CJ never re-entered the picture, and that I turned away from situations that I knew, deep down inside of me, were not healthy. The truth is that although Forward Moving provided all the tools I needed to help me navigate through the rocky waters that awaited, they could not provide the map that would help me avoid them.

The months and years following graduation would find me changing careers, close to the brink of death once more, in new romantic relationships, and trying to bring to fruition a lifelong dream. Self-doubt and insecurities would continue to be formidable competitors for my new skill set to face.

But, having a new skill set to call upon and use would be the cornerstones on which I would be able to carve out a happier life for myself. It wouldn't be easy. It wouldn't be overnight. It would, however, be possible.

Good or bad, life itself is our reward. At a certain point we can take control over what and whom we allow in our world, and we don't owe an explanation for the decisions we make on our own behalf. For three months, I pressed the pause button on my life. I let go of the fear that held me captive in order to embrace and have faith in my ability to steer my life in the direction I chose.

It was with the skills I was taught that I would finally be able to *Press Play*.

Acknowledgements

Having a family and people who surround, love, and believe in me in spite of myself is what has made this book possible.

My mother Ronnie, the epitome of beauty and bravery. From day one, it has been you and me against the world—side by side, hand in hand, heart to heart, soul to soul. Thank you for entrusting me to tell our family's story.

Kayla, my intelligent, beautiful daughter, who challenges me, inspires me, and holds me accountable. You will always be the best moment of my life. Your love makes me want to be a better woman than I was the day before.

Aunt Kathy, who taught me that courage is found in even the youngest soul. And if that soul is attached to a beautiful heart, then those who are loved by it will never go unprotected.

Chris and Rob, who believed me and in me. You never wavered, never questioned, and never doubted. To be the sister of two good men is not only a blessing, but continues to give me hope.

Maryann and Jeanmarie, whose arms and doors have always

been open. You never judged me or stopped my brothers from being there for me. You simply loved me. You are the sisters I always wanted.

My beautiful cousin Patti, whose resilience and strength have no limits. When I wonder if I possess the ability to push through, you are my reminder that we are capable of overcoming anything.

The women who left too soon: Grandma Katie, whose pure heart and innocence will never be matched by another. You taught me everything I ever needed to know about kindness by simply being yourself. I love you, doll. Aunt Mickey, who was the most difficult and complicated human being I have ever known—I now understand. Aunt Ellen, whose abuse prevented her from seeing the intelligent and worthy woman she was. My cousin Erin, who taught me the most painful lesson of all: never put off till tomorrow what you can say today, because tomorrow may be too late.

Mike. You answered the phone that morning. You showed up. You didn't have to. You may not have even wanted to, but you did. I will always be grateful.

Ann Fiorentino Rosenberg. Two young girls just trying to save each other from those who tried to destroy them. You saw in me all the things I never believed existed. You were my lifeline. My life would have been much lonelier and more isolated if not for you. Time and distance may keep us apart, but the love and gratitude I hold in my heart, my soul, keeps you with me every day.

Christine and Arielle. All my life I prayed in one way or another for someone like both of you to find and rescue me. I thank God for answering those prayers and finding a way to get me to you.

Joanne Colella. You were the very first person who told me that I was a writer. Through the years, as I wrote and shared little stories on Facebook, you would send me a message and ask, "When are you writing the book, Maureen?" I can finally answer, "Here it is, my friend." Thank you, always, for your friendship, faith and persistence.

Jenn Tuma-Young. I always hoped to write this story. And, when I did I thought I wrote it well. That's when you walked in. You thought it was good, but believed . . . KNEW . . . it could be better. You carefully guided me in order to make it a great and important story I am now proud to tell. You pulled truths and memories I was afraid to put on paper, and helped me shed the shame and fear. We laughed and cried, and walked hand in hand, page by page. There are no words to adequately thank you. I am forever grateful to you, not only as the incredible publisher you are but for the beautiful friend you have become to me. I can't wait to do it all over again with you.

You are all the strongest threads in the tapestry of my life.

ACKNOWLEDGEMENTS

You held on tight to me and refused to let go. You are why I have hope and believe in magic. My love and thanks are infinite.

About the Author

A born and bred Brooklyn girl, Maureen Spataro resides in New Jersey where she has lived since 1992, and is the proud mother of Kayla, who was recently inducted into the New Jersey BAR.

In addition to being the founder of the non-profit organization Because She Is, Maureen is a NJ real estate agent and contributing writer for BELLA Magazine

As a survivor of multiple traumas, Maureen hopes that by sharing her story a better understanding of a survivor's perspective will open up an honest conversation among family members and peers, as well as the public as a whole.

To connect with Maureen, visit her website: http://becausesheis.org

To download a playlist of the songs mentioned in this book, visit: http://becausesheis.org/press-pause-playlist

CPSIA information can be obtained
at www.ICGtesting.com
Printed in the USA
BVHW061007070422
633677BV00003B/201

9 780578 659329